THE ZEN
OF LIFE, LIES, AND ABERRANT REALITY

FURTHER ZEN RAMBLINGS FROM THE INTERNET

SCOTT SHAW

Buddha Rose Publications

The Zen of Life, Lies, and Aberrant Reality
Copyright © 2015 by Scott Shaw
All Rights Reserved
www.scottshaw.com

No Part of this book may be reproduced in any manner without the expressed written permission of the author or the publishing company.

Rear cover of photograph of Scott Shaw by Hae Won Shin.
Copyright © 2015 All Rights Reserved.

First Edition 2015

ISBN 10: 1-877792-80-2
ISBN 13: 9781877792809

Library of Congress: 2015931591

Printed in the United States of America

10 9 8 7 6 5 4 3 2 1

THE ZEN
OF LIFE, LIES, AND ABERRANT REALITY

Introduction

Well, here it is, *The Scott Shaw Zen Blog 4.0,* originally presented for your reading pleasure on the World Wide Web @ scottshaw.com. All of the writings presented in this book were written between September 2014 and January of 2015.

As was the case with the previously published volumes based upon *The Scott Shaw Zen Blog;* entitled: *Scribbles on the Restroom Wall*, *The Chronicles: Zen Ramblings from the Internet*, and *Words in the Wind,* this volume is presented exactly as it was viewed on scottshaw.com, with no rewriting, punctuation, or typo corrections. From this, we hope you will receive the original reading experience.

This volume of internet ramblings, similar to *Words in the Wind,* is presented with the date and time listed as to when each blog was originally posted. Also, the blogs in this volume are presented from end to beginning, as opposed to *Scribbles on the Restroom Wall* and *The Chronicles: Zen Ramblings from the Internet*, that were presented from beginning to end. With this, we hope to present a transcendence back through time as opposed to an evolving evolution. In addition, we left out the traditional *Table of Contents* and the manuscript is presented in an unpaginated format. Thus, hopefully, leaving this volume as a much more free-flowing reading experience.

Okay, there's the information and the definitions. Read on… We hope you enjoy it. And, be sure to stayed tuned for the ongoing *Scott Shaw Zen Blog* at scottshaw.com.

That was a Mistake

20/January/2015 15:48

Have you ever had the experience of being in the process of doing something and you realize that it is a mistake but because the action is already in motion you have no choice but to continue forward with it? I think most of us have encountered moments like that in our life. Hopefully, there are not a lot of them but in each case they can come to define the rest of our existence.

The mistakes we make can be large or they can be small. They can involve our choosing to be involved with a specific person or group. They can be actions that we are guided into by others. They can be actions that we choose to make on our own. Or, they can simply be accidents of fate. But, in each case, the mistake can alter our life. Once we realize that we have made the mistake it is only us who is left to deal with the consequences. Even if others are involved, it is we, as individuals, who must pay the individual price.

I think most people, if they are honest with themselves and look to their life, will each view things that they just should not have done and knew they should not be doing while they were doing it. Some people, however, once they make a mistake, lie about it, hide from the consequences, and try to justify their actions. That is simply the wrong mindset to possess. For, if you can't be honest with yourself and present that honesty to the world, no level of denying your actions will ever cleanse yours sins.

Life is an ongoing process beginning with birth and ending with death. During that short period of time, no one is perfect, no one has not done something wrong, no one has not made mistakes. The thing that sets the conscious person apart from the disingenuous individual is the person who recognizes their mistakes, sees them for what they are, and moves towards fixing all that has been broken by their choices and their actions.

If you want to been seen as a conscious person, own your mistakes and then fix your mistakes. Whatever it takes, that is what must be done.

Precepts and Patterns

20/January/2015 09:07

The life of each person is defined by a unique set of precepts and patterns. They do what they do and they follow a prescribed pathway throughout their life. Many believe that they change and evolve throughout time. But, this is not the case. Though certain physical aspects may change in a person's life; for example where they go to school, where they work, where they live, if they get married, if they come to have children, and so on, the precepts and the patterns of their life does not change. This pattern of defined patterns is locked into the subconscious of all people.

If you follow a person throughout their life you will see that there is a very specific pattern that defines all of their actions and interactions. Some people are much more obsessive compulsive than others. Meaning, they form a pattern of doing a specific thing at a specific time and hold tightly onto it. Others appear more free-flowing with their life patterns but, none-the-less, that too is a prescribed definition in their life, thus a precept and a pattern.

It is for this reason that people constantly make the same mistakes over and over and over again. They do the same things that comes to define their life in a negative way. They interact with people using the same interactive strategy that they have become comfortless with and, thus, are left with less than ideal relationships. They do they same things that cause them to be physically or mentally unhealthy and are then left with the consequences.

For those who live a positive, productive, plentiful life, this is also the cause. Their set of defining precepts and patterns works in a manner where they attract people who help not hinder their life and, from this, are called to move up the ladder of life as they have a set of precepts and patterns that others find helpful.

All individual psychological characteristics are also defined by individual precepts and patterns: be it a person who is kind, helpful, and giving, or someone who is egotistical, deceitful, insecure, or vengeful.

Precepts and patterns are set and a person follows them throughout their life. Though slight alterations may be made to them if an individually forcefully takes hold of their consciousness, that too is defined by their previously determined precepts and patterns.

You are who you are. What you are has already been defined. But, it is you who can choose to do what you want with your precepts and patterns. My advice, clearly define your precepts and patterns and make them work to your advantage not to your detriment.

The Facts in Artistic Portrayals

19/January/2015 14:20

If you watch the new film, *Selma,* you will see that the filmmaker, Ava DuVernay, portrays President Lyndon B. Johnson as walking hand-in-hand with J. Edgar Hoover in preparing a sex tape and sending it to Martin Luther King, Jr. and his wife presenting MLK's infidelities. Historically, that is simply wrong. LBJ had nothing to do with it. Also incorrect is that the film depicts that LBJ was not one-hundred percent in favor of *The Voting Rights Act of 1965.* Though MLK and LBJ had a slightly different timetable, history shows that LBJ was the instrumental force in getting that bill passed.

I have heard interviews with DuVernay where she states this film is not a documentary, thus she has artistic license to alter the truth. But, is that right to do? When you make a film and use a true, not fictional person, I believe that you have the obligation to depict that person with absolute truth. It is not right to alter historical facts or to take a person words or actions out of context or to portray them in any false manner simply to make a film more compelling to watch. This is especially the case when the film is supposedly a fact-based production.

In this day and age, most people never look to the history books – they never study historical records. All they do is see a film or read a blog and believe every word that they hear.

From a person perspective, people have made supposed documentaries and/or have written and published articles and chapters in books about me that were completely riddled with incorrect facts or misquoted, misaligned, statements. People see it, people read it, and people believe it. I cannot tell you how many times someone has come up to me and asked me about something that someone else stated that I did or I said and I have no idea what they are talking about. When I inquire as to the source, I can categorically state that what they said was wrong. Yet, no one ever takes anything back. So, people are still out there believing.

Let's fact it, that is just wrong. Just like it is wrong to portray a person of historical substance in a less than truthful light.

People lie. People are motivated by their own motivations whenever they speak about another person. Believe that first before you believe anything else.

The point being, LBJ or MLK are not here to stand up and answer back to their portrayal in this film. Now, I am all about getting the message out there about what took place in the South and how the dominant vicious people held back the African-Americans for no good reason, with only racism as a basis. But, I believe it should be done in a truthful and honest manner. The facts should never be fabricated. Enough bad things were done by enough bad people that you do not have to twist history to make a movie worth watching.

Oblivious or I Just Don't Care

19/January/2015 13:43

I was pulling into the parking lot this morning at *The Original Farmer's Market* to get my morning eats on before going to a Production Meeting in Burbank. To get in you have to push a button, pull a ticket, wait for the gate to rise, and then go in. Me, I pulled up, pushed the button, got my ticket, the gate goes up, but I cannot enter as there is this old guy completely blocking my passageway, as he wants this one particular parking spot. The problem is, there is a lady putting her baby in the child seat of her SUV -- meaning, all this is going to take a long time. I honk. The old guy looks, but does nothing. The car behind me honks. The guy again looks, he still does nothing. He is not going to move until he gets that one parking spot. This, when there are tons of other spots just down the row. Finally, instead of getting out of my car and screaming at the old mutha fucka to move, I inch my way behind his car, go down the wrong way, just to get in. What an unconscious asshole!

Yesterday, I was on my way to having breakfast over in the LBC. To get to the restaurant I have to drive down this one-way street. Normally, all-good but yesterday there is a guy who has planted his car in the middle of the street waiting for a parking spot. The problem in this case was, the spot he was waiting for was held by a guy who had his gym bag on the top of his trunk. He was looking through it. Then, he answers a phone call. He was not going to go anywhere anytime soon. Me, after witnessing all this, I give a polite honk to the guy in the car just to let him know there were people behind him. Finally, he pulls over a little bit. I squeeze past him. As I do, he flips me off. I stop my car to see what he will do next, planning to get out and kick his ass. I mean, he is the one doing something wrong and he flips me off. Hello! My lady got me focused, however, and told me to just let it go. She was right. They guy did nothing else. So, I drove on.

In life, this is the thing... We are frequently confronted by people who are either oblivious or who just do not care about the affect they are having on other people. Are you one of them? The thing is, these are the people who mess everything up. They are the one's who ruin the lives of other people. Sure, maybe you can be patient or pretend to be patient, but as long as they are doing what they are doing, not thinking about others before they do what they do, they are messing with people's lives. And, this is simply wrong.

And, this doesn't just go to the driving experience. It goes to all aspects of life.

The fact is, this is life and we are going to encounter people who create situations like the one's I just described all the time. It's not right but it is the way it is. The only thing we can do is to not be those people.

If we always take other people into consideration, then the world becomes just a little bit better.

If You Don't Know Then You Don't Know
19/January/2015 08:34

    I think it is very curious how people continually project their own definition onto another person. They believe that they know who a person is and why they are doing what they are doing. The main point is, they never know. Another person can never truly know what someone else is thinking or why he or she is doing what they are doing unless they truly know that person and then, in many cases, they still cannot truly know.

    Much of life is defined by our need to draw conclusions. Some people are much more fervent about this process than others. Some people immediately cast their decisions onto what others are saying or doing and why they are saying an doing it. But, by living life in this manner the truth and suchness of other people are forever lost.

    In life, somethings we are forced into drawing conclusions about a person's actions and/or motivations. In these incidences, this is generally brought about by the other person them-self. They do something that forces our hand; whether that be something physical, verbal, or sneaky, we must come to a conclusion to protect our own being.

    Here we see how much of life is lived at the most animalistic level. For conclusions and reactions were instigated by someone else's bad behavior or their negative interaction with life and with us. Thus, we must do something to keep their doing from damaging us any further.

    Most of life is not like this, however. Most of life is quite passive. We live, we do, we make choices defined by our own set of circumstances, and that is that. This being said, there are still those who want to cast their own definition onto other people and in some cases project these definitions onto the world. Are you one of these people? If you are, not only are you robbing the life of the person you are casting your judgments upon but you are taking away any sense of spontaneity and freedom form your own existence.

    You are not All-Knowing. No one is. Stop acting like you are.

The Music is Getting Old

19/January/2015 08:25

There was an interesting set of music presentations over this past weekend. This one cable station presented live concerts from a number of very well-know performers. The first one I took notice of was Neil Young.

In this concert/documentary about Neil, he was playing in Toronto, near his hometown. Neil took to the stage playing both acoustic and electric guitar He did this solo, with no band. This struck me as very strange and almost made me feel uncomfortable, for here was Neil Young with his trademark Les Paul and Gretsch completely rockin' as if he were supported by a band. Normally, when you think of a solo performance from someone like Neil Young he would be unplugged and singing with one of his acoustic Martins or at the piano. But, here he was solo, blasting rock n' roll. Strange…

It made me think back to when I was a teenager. I would be sitting in my room playing Neil Young songs with my *Gibson SG* with a *Bigsby* tailpiece through my *Fender Blender* and *Acoustic* amp thinking how much better it would be with a band. But, there was Neil Young performing some of the same songs I played way back then; and doing them just as I had played them, alone. Curious…

Mostly, Neil Young looked so old.

Two of the other bands that were featured were *Duran Duran* and *Depeche Mode.* My lady, a big fan of *Duran Duran,* watched their whole performance. I couldn't bring myself to do it. I did watch some of *Depeche Mode,* however. (Some, not all). Afterwards, all my lady could say was, *"They all look so old."*

The network also did a show with *Garbage.* I always wondered how, Butch Vig, a Super-Producer, ever had the time to do *Garbage.* But, the first thing I noticed was how old Shirley Manson looked.

It was like I joking stated to one of my LP record shopping buddies a while back when we were talking about this one singer, *"It's one thing to watch a girl perform in her twenties, it's another thing when they are in their fifties."*

Now, I'm not putting these people down because Neil is older but the rest are my age-ish. It is just that when you look to the trends in music, it is getting old. The remaining Beatles and the Stones are in their seventies. The Punk, New Wave, and first generation Hip-Hop people are in their middle to late fifties and into their sixties. Even those of the Grunge and Boy Band eras are deep in their forties or older.

Sure, sure, new music and new musicians come along all the time. But, until a new music genre takes hold all we are left with is TV that demonstrates how old music is getting.

Telling Lies

18/January/2015 08:59

It always surprises me when someone tells a lie about another person.

Have you ever had someone tell a lie about you?

Have you ever told a lie about someone else?

I am sure there are deep-rooted psychological issues in any person who finds it necessary to tell a lie about another person. I am also sure that the majority of the people who make up lies about another person feel that they have a reason to do so. This being the case, telling a lie about another person is never justified in your logic, mental programming, or psychological framework.

A lie is a lie is a lie.

Why do people tell lies about another person? It is generally to discredit or damage the life or livelihood of that person. As this is the foundational factor, the questions must be asked, *"Who are you to judge?"* And, *"Who are you to feel you have the right to take that action?"*

Lies can be small, such as rearranging the thoughts, words, or actions of a person and then presenting your presentation to the world. Or, they can be large, such as completely fabricating a tale about an individual. Small or large, the outcome is the same; people may believe what you have said. If they do believe the lie you told that means you have set an entire chain of events in motion based upon a falsehood. As you are the instigator, whatever the outcome, you are responsible for that end.

Whatever is born in deception can never emerge with a positive outcome. Thus, as you have been the instigator and the cause of the deception, negativity will seek you out.

The fact is, when someone tells a lie about another person they are usually so wrapped up in their own emotional mindset – a state of mind of thinking only about themselves, that they are not looking towards the future. All·they are thinking about is the immediacy of the now. Here lies the problem, whenever you are lost in the emotions of the moment, you are separated from Clear Mind and, as such, you are only embracing the Lower Self. Whenever the Lower Self is the sourcepoint of your actions, negative events occur. Whether you care about the larger overall outcome in that moment or not, your words and your actions are what sets the next level of your life evolution in motion. What you say and do today equals your tomorrow.

Lying about someone may give you a momentary feeling of empowerment. It may even allow you to damage the life of that individual. But, the presentation of a lie, no matter how small or how extravagant, is never the truth. Sooner or later your lie will be uncovered and whatever momentary sense of accomplishment and power you may have felt, while damaging the life of another, will be unveiled and you will be seen for what you truly are.

Who do you want to be? A person who spread good and truth throughout the world or one who lies about others eventually suffering the consequences of your own words and deeds?

Who Do You Care About and Why?

16/January/2015 08:39

I often find it very curious how the majority of the world's people only think about themselves. Even when they are supposedly thinking about somebody or something else they are thinking about them or it from a very personal perspective. *"This is my cause." "What that person, that corporation, that political entity is doing makes me angry."*

When actions are taken due to emotion they are not *Pure Action,* they are only *Reactionary Action. Reactionary Action* never is based upon a true sense of caring or giving; it is only based upon the temporary randomness of emotion.

Emotion is the source for the majority of the world's problems and all of the bad things that take place all across the globe. *"I feel this way so I react and I do that." "I want this and I don't care who I harm in getting it." "I feel this way and everybody and the whole world be damned! I am going to express how I feel!" "That person is wrong and I am going to mess them up."* And so on...

Here lies one of the biggest problems with much of modern society – people are told that they have the right to feel what they feel and do what they what to do based upon those feelings. People are told, and thus they believe, that they have the right to do anything that they feel like doing. That is what you have been told and how you feel; right? The moment this misplaced understanding is questioned, war erupts. This is the source point for where this world gets very messy.

If we look to some of the most simply examples of this we can see how personal actions expands to global devastation. A person is driving. They come up to a stoplight. They start checking their phone for messages. The light turns green and the people behind them start honking. The driver initially doesn't hear them honking because they are enthralled in reading their messages. The honking and perhaps yelling continues. Finally, the driver realizes the light is green so they start to move but instead of feeling sorry for hindering the life of another person, they are mad because someone else honked at them. This goes on all the time and it a couple of instances I have seen actual fights break out due to it.

This was just one example. People do selfish things that negatively affect the life of other people all the time. Do they care? In most cases, they do not. They only care about what they are feeling when they are feeling it.

Think about this, how many times have you been locked into doing something – how many times have you been feeling an emotion, and you react because of it. How many of those times has someone else suffered the consequences due to you only thinking about yourself? Now, this action may have even been motivate by what you believe is an altruistic mindset but if others are negatively affected that means what you were feeling, equally what you were doing, has hurt someone else. What do you think is the life reaction to that? Who should be held responsible?

People only care about their own moment. This is the way most people behave throughout their life but it does not have to be the way you behave. Be more, think about others first, and the world becomes a better place.

The Negativity of Micro-Periods

15/January/2015 09:05

Life is broken up into particular micro-periods. In one specific period we encounter a specific type of person or life events. Why this is, is anybody's guess. But, if nothing else, it allows us to learn from life and from the actions of other people.

Recently, I've had a few curious encounters while shopping. Yesterday, I walked into a bookstore. Immediately, near the entrance I heard this guy talking to himself. I took note of him and moved on. A bit later, I could see that he was apparently calculating his purchase. He went into a rank, *"Fuck, fuck, fuck, shit, shit, shit."* Then, he looked around and noticed that people were looking at him, (or were trying not to look at him), so he went into the Irish version of shit, *"Shite, shite, shite."*

I assumed that he didn't have enough money for his desired purchased. I would have been happy to throw him a couple of dollars but as he was obviously mentally ill and off his meds I decided it was probably best not to interact with him. Let his own melodrama play out as it will.

All this set me to thinking about personal interaction. Me, being who (and what) I am, I encounter a lot of people. Maybe that interaction only takes place for a couple of moments but I do meet a lot of people. And, I have long realized that most people are very nice. They are who they are, they do what they do, and like them or not, they exist in the same time-space as me. All good…

Some people, however, project a very specific persona. Certainly, the mentally ill, off their meds, are an exaggerated example. But, some of the others are the very egotistical, the all-knowing, the self-righteous, the overbearing, the macho, and so on. On the other side of the spectrum, some are the very meek and insecure. All of these attributes can be traced back to personality and psychological programing but I find those that embrace negativity the most curious for what is the benefit of being a negative person?

…I speak of this because I have been also encountering a few very negative types over the past several days.

Have you ever met a person and the minute you begin to speak with them they project an abundance of negativity. This can be projected in the form of the aforementioned personality traits but over-riding them is this source essence of negativity. When I take note of this trait in people I often try to peer deeply into the who of what they are, in order to try to figure out from where it arises. It may be personality or psychologically programing, as in the other cases of exaggerated personality, but with negativity the source is so much more damning because by encountering the world in that manner, not only do they drive people away but they drive life-possibilities away. So, why do it? Does it somehow make them feel better or more? I don't know?

Perhaps the most interesting case-studies of those who embrace negativity, that I have encountered, are those who pretend to be very happy go lucky and positive people, yet in their soul, negativity rules. It always takes awhile to peel back the layers of personality, in this specific personality, for their true inner-nature to be revealed. But, these are very few and far between. Mostly, the negative are very negative.

In life, for those of us who care, I think we always question, *"Why?"* This is the case especially when we encounter a person embracing negativity. But, in many case, "Why," is the answer. For these people who live life, embracing this predilection of energy, either do not know or do not care about the effect it is having on them and the world around them. Thus, they are trapped as a conduit of negativity.

Ultimately, you can never change a person; they can only change themselves if they care to do so. So, all you can do is protect yourself, stand back, and let the people who embrace negativity play out their own melodrama without you being a part of it.

Knowing that you can never truly change a person, it is essential to keep your distance from this type of person by not allowing their actions and reactions to affect yours. For negativity only equals negativity and no excuse they make for their behavior or actions is ever valid when their behavior or actions negatively affects your life.

Be safe. Be positive.

On Their Soapbox

14/January/2015 09:34

I was walking through *The Mission District* in San Francisco last weekend. The only reason I ever go to The Mission is because there is this great two-story thrift store located there. I rarely ever buy anything at the shop, but whenever I'm in SF I hit over there to check out the sights and the sounds because they have some really unique stuff.

As I walked through The Mission with all of its crazies, its hookers, its drug dealers, its gang bangers, its homeless, its violent offenders, its very dirty sidewalks, its stench, I looked over to my lady and said, *"If there is a hell, this is what it is like."* The innate tension in The Mission is very high.

Amusingly, we saw this one young Chinese woman, obviously a SF local, but a local from the better side of town. She stood there looking around lost. She wore very fashionable clothing, high boots, style haired, and she carried a small high-quality paper bag. You know the kind where a little tissue paper is coming out of the top. It was obviously a gift and she was on her way to some sort of a baby shower, bridal shower, or housewarming in hell. But, she wasn't quite sure how to get there.

You could tell she was made nervous by her surroundings. When she saw my lady and I, obviously also not Mission locals, she began to walk very close to us. I smiled inside. That was AOK with me, if she needs a little help and security, I was happy to provide it.

I always smile in environments like this. For they are not so different from where I grew up. All the macho tension. All the men walking with swagger. All the yelling across the street at one another and at nobody in particular. I often wonder how those city boys who think they are all bad-assed would survive in an environment like this. They would be stomped. Anyone who walks with swagger doesn't have any swagger.

Anyway...

On one corner was this guy preaching the gospel very loudly in Spanish. He was yelling about La Muerte, Jesus

Christo, and all the etc. But, no one was listening. All he was doing was disturbing and already disturbed environment.

I remember as a kid in downtown L.A. how I had seen this same scenario so many times. Always a different person but always someone screaming, telling people that they were sinners and that they needed to repent. ...They needed to live the way this person was telling them they should live.

Me, I pulled out my digital tape recorder and taped a little bit of his dialogue. I will use it in some piece of music later on down the line.

But, to the point... All those who scream about their knowledge... All those who tell people what is going to happen to them, if... All those who tell people how they should live and do it loudly -- all they are trying to do is make themselves something that that they not. For if they were that, all they would have to do is BE. Their being would be enough to help those around them.

People scream out because they are insecure in their own knowledge. People scream out because they want to be seen as something grand and holy. But, if they were grand or holy they would not be screaming out at all because grandness and holiness is silent. Grandness and holiness is not defined by a person's ego telling them that they have something worth saying and from this find the motivation to stand on a street corner, or wherever else, and yell at people how they should live and what they should be doing. That's not imparting knowledge, that's just ego.

But, as stated, if there is a hell, The Mission is what it would be like. And, as all ego does is drive a person to hell, I guess that street corner preacher was in the right place. :-)

Conflict, Guerrilla Warfare, and Unrequited Love
13/January/2015 15:12

OUT: I went out today to teach a class for advanced black belts. The class was for three men and one of them asked if his teenage son could join in. Though not a novice, as he had trained with his father, he was still very new to the game. But, of course, he was invited in with open arms.

It's been years since I've taught new martial artists. But, I think back to when I ran a school and in many ways that is the most rewarding thing to do; usher a student into the world of martial arts and all of its benefits.

My definition of a martial arts master is not someone who can do everything well but someone who knows what they personally can do very well. This class was the ideal example of that. Sure, all three of the black belts knew the drills but there they were working on their own continued development while instructing the son. I could see how each of the members was embracing their own unique understanding of the fighting arts and showing it to the young man. This is what I consider an ideal class and the perfect training ground for the advanced and the new practitioner alike – learning while teaching.

After the class I decided to do a thrift store run on my way home, as you never know what you will find. At my first stop I came upon a collection of rare, Jamaica pressing, reggae. The known stuff like Bob Marley and Peter Tosh were all scratched to hell, I left them behind, but the obscure stuff like *The Heptones* and *Greyhound* were clean-clean-clean. I bought them all.

While I was looking at the vinyl this whole conflict took place behind me. A lady who entered the store, who was apparently not supposed to be in the store (for whatever reason) was told by the female manager that she was not allowed to shop in the store. The lady went off. *"I can be wherever I want to be! Fuck you! What kind of manger are you? Trying to be all perfect and shit!"* It went on and on. Then she went around to all the customers, angrily asking, *"Why do you shop here? This store is terrible! Look at they way they treat me!"* Etc., etc., etc… Thankfully, she didn't come up to me.

Finally, with the threat of police action and her not following through with, *"You want to fight me bitch?"* She walked towards the door. It came to an end.

This store was in *the hood,* okay... But, wherever it was, most people don't behave like that. There is just no reason for it...

I paid for the LPs, hit for the car, and was heading over to another thrift store en route home. On the radio I heard about this guy who made millions on the internet, developing some sort of socially conscious program, but then was arrested for trying to hire a hitman on the web to kill somebody he didn't like. Okay... Bit of a dichotomy there...

It made me realize how the internet is such a playground for guerrilla warfare. I mean people do all this shit, talk all this shit, but they do it while hiding behind their computer screen. I thought back to the class I taught today. There was a group of people who got out there and actually did something positive with their life. They spent their time learning and mastering the martial arts. From this, they can teach others the ancient understandings of physical and mental refinement. They don't sit around at a keyboard and try to damage the lives of other people. I mean, if they needed to they could go hand-to-hand. But, that's just it, because they can, they are secure in themselves and do not have to live at the lower levels of mind fuck bullshit that so many people who live their whole life on the internet are prone to. My advice, get out there and do something physically and mentally positive with your life that will actually mean something. Do something positive for the world. Stop the negative internet bullshit. It begins with you!

At my final stop, I was walking around and this lady was taking very loudly on her cell phone. She was screeching at a guy, *"I know there was feelings between us! I know it! I could tell when you made love to me! Now, you're telling me it's nothing! You're lying! I know you care about me!"* Okay...

You know... I so often would like to explain to women before they do what they do; a lot of men just want sex so they say whatever it is they have to say to get it but then once it has been gotten, they are in the wind. Hit it and quit it just to say they did it... Be careful.

Life is this crazy messed up mess. People seek conflict because they have nothing better to do. If you are doing something better, you don't seek it, because you are fulfilled onto yourself. You don't need to create controversy in public, you don't need to do bad things that will get you band from shopping at a store, you don't need to challenge anybody to a fight, you don't need to mess with people on the internet, you don't need to lie to people simply to fulfill your bodily desire, and you don't need to prove anything because you are whole onto yourself.

Be more with you life. Do something more.

Me, after all that, I stopped at the shoreline and looked out to the divine mother ocean for a time. I needed her peaceful embrace.

Cameras Are Everywhere

12/January/2015 10:18

I was up in San Francisco filming a couple scenes for an upcoming movie. I decided to hit over to Berkeley, across the bay, to catch some lunch at this great Pho restaurant. Afterwards I went to this bookstore, that I just love, to check out what they had on tap.

I found that they had this great selection of books on Sufism published in the Middle East – very rare to find books like that. Me, I have been a lover of rare books forever. It is kind of a funny experience when you realize that you have been doing something for longer than most people have been alive. Remember that when you get there...

Anyway, these books were housed at the end of a book isle. I was enthralled, but down at the far end of the isle I had heard some people making kind of inappropriate remarks for a bookstore – making fun of titles and stuff. No big deal, I looked and they were some young people, in their early twenties, so I didn't think much more about it. Back to being hypnotized...

Maybe ten or fifteen minutes later, I continued to hear some commotion from these people, but it had been ongoing so I never lost my focus on the books. Finally, I looked and at the end of the isle they had set up a large *Betacam* on a *Sachtler* tripod. They were probably students from *Cal*, filming a student film or where about to. I laughed to myself and left the isle; didn't want to be filmed.

You know, I used to hate it when the Age of Paparazzi was new here in L.A. and they'd be around filming celebrities and wanta-be celebrities everywhere. Or, when people would be taking my photograph without asking. Now, everybody has a *GoPro*, a camera phone, a whatever... And, everywhere you go they are taking your picture. I've just given into the reality of reality. As long as they are cool about it, I don't get pissed any more.

As I walked away the cast and crew were all looking at me. I guess the way I was dressed or looked (especially in Berkeley): long blonde hair and purple tinted Oliver Peoples glasses; they knew I was somebody (or something) but couldn't decide which. :-)

The funny thing I thought, as I walked away, is that if they had filmed me and then shown their piece to their class or the large audiences they usually draw in for those senior screening, is that someone would have recognized me and wondered, *"How did you get Max Hell in your movie?"* :-)

Awh, life and cameras... I just can't get away from 'em.

Bullshit, Buffoonery, and the What is Your End-Game
12/January/2015 10:17

I was kicking around Santa Cruz, as I frequently do, and I walked past this one psychic who is always set up on this one street. Whenever I walk by, he looks up from his client and makes eye contact with me. I always smile back at him and nod. He knows that I know... But, I will get to that in a moment.

Back in the late 60s and through the 70s; even into the early 80s, Santa Cruz was a magnet for spiritual types. I too ponder moving there when I was off to college. I went as far as to look for a cabin to rent up in the Santa Cruz Mountains. But, for whatever karmic reason, I stayed in L.A. I guess that was a good thing because a year to two later there was a torrential downpour and many of those cabins were lost to massive mudslides and flooding, along with the people in them.

I have long charted, (and have written about), how so many of the spiritually-based people I knew that moved up to Santa Cruz became total vegs as the time when on. I would see them leave and a few years later, if I bumped into them, they were total space cases. Why does Santa Cruz do that to a person? Or, is it the person doing it to themselves? I don't know...

As I walked down the street, a couple of days ago, I saw this one guy: long beard, long hair, draw sting pants – looked like the total spiritual type that came out of the 70s. If he were there, then, he would have totally fit in. Now, the world has changed. This guy, who was probably in his late twenties, was/is nothing but a burn out. He sat on the street pondering whatever reality he was lost in. But, he was doing nothing with his life.

I have to wonder what is the call of Santa Cruz in this day and age, as all these hippie-types keep showing up. But, showing up to what? I knew what the call was back then. But, then is not now. Now, the Santa Cruz Mountains are filled with high-priced homes built by programmers who work over the hill in Silicon Valley. The people no longer go there for spirituality, because there is none. So, why do they go there and burn out?

And, I think this is one of the things that we all have to think about in life, *"What is our End-Game?" "Why are we doing what we are doing?"* If we don't know, then we don't know… You really need to know, because if you don't know, you can end up a burn out.

Okay… Now, back to the psychic, who makes his bucks by setting up a small table with two chairs on the street. The guy is probably in his sixties. He most likely showed up in Santa Cruz way back in the way back when. Was his mission to be a street corner psychic?

Some times when I walk past him I hear him doing what all psychic do… They do this thing where they initially ask probing questions and then by studying your body language, your eye movement, and your responses, they figure out where your sweet-spot is. From there, they go after it?

"What do you want to know?" "What are looking to find out?" "Has someone close to you passed on?" "I feel there is someone trying to contact you." Or, the big-banger, *"I feel there is a spirit following you."* Bullshit and Buffoonery! But, people still go to these people. Especially in a place like Santa Cruz. This guy always has people at his table.

For the record, I too (for shits & giggles) have gone to psychics. In one case, the person was a very prominent psychic. But, they always get it wrong. Not one time could they tell me anything but BS. And, here's the thing, my autobiography has already been written. My life is out there for the public to read. Plus, I am a very open person; you ask, I tell. So, in two of the aforementioned psychic experiences, I could tell someone had read up on me and tried to pull that stuff out of their hat. But, though the physical aspects of my life are out there, and what I think about what I think about, are out there – that is not the inner me. They always got it wrong!

And, when a psychic tries to pull the, *"There's a person's spirit who is following you,"* out of their deck of cards, let's think about that… In life, there is two defining factors. You will live and you will die. That is fact. Why would one specific person have the ability to decide to stick around, either to help or to haunt you? Sure, sure, there is all kinds of bullshit talked and written about on that subject; the why and they wherefores…

But, it is all one of three things: speculation, people trying to make a buck, or one of the number one facts of life; people lie.

The fact is, you ask three, *"Experts,"* on the subject and you will get three different answers. Thus, there is no one truth. There are only certain people believing that they know. But, what do they know? Nothing! At best, they believe their own lies.

The reality is, you live, you die, and you try to live the best life you can between those two definitive factors. End of story!

The more you buy into the bullshit, the more the bullshit controls your life. And, the more money you have the potential to give to people who hang out on the street in Santa Cruz and charge you to tell your future.

Be free. Know you. Pursue you and what you want. Know your End-Game. But, don't let people who are only trying to make a buck dominate your life-space.

Making Yourself Relevant

09/January/2015 20:15

I caught a few minutes of TMZ this evening. On it, this one TMZ guy went up to the Reverend Al Sharpton and told him about the fact that the actor James Woods had apparently gone on at rank against Sharpton on Twitter. Now, I don't tweet, so I don't know anything about the particulars of all that. But, Sharpton's response was funny. He initially asked, *"Does he still act?"* Then he went on to say, in essence, *"If talking about me is going to make you revenant and get you another job, talk about me all you want!"* His discourse went on for a few minutes. Very funny…

Now, I have no feelings for Sharpton or Woods one way or the other. Though Woods did ask me for a light for his cigar one night out in front of one of my favorite restaurant of all time that went RIP in 2014, *Kate Mantilinis*.

But, the point Sharpton made was very valid. People do that kind of stuff all the time. They talk about others, try to get people riled up in order to make themselves seem like some all-knowing source and make themselves feel empowered. They do it to make themselves appear relevant. They hope that word will spread about the words they speak. But, the words they speak are not based upon individual creation or philosophy; they are about someone else. And, when your words are about someone else, you owe that person of whom you speak everything, for it was what they did or what they said, and you making comment on them, that is making people take notice of you.

The fact is, and this is something I have said forever, if you are talking about someone else that means you don't have anything of your own worth saying.

In life, we each have our opinions about what is taking place in our life, the world around us, and what other people are doing. Nothing wrong with that… But, there are some people who try to move themselves into the foreground by actually spreading their opinions to the world. And, as we all know, most people are very discontent with their life; they are looking for a reason to be upset. So, it is very easy to work people up into a frenzy if you start spreading negative statements about a person. And, people do this whether their words are based upon fact or fiction.

Fact: Opinions are not truth, opinion are only opinions.

Fact: If you are spreading negative opinions all you are doing is making this Life-Place worst not better.

If you want to be truly relevant, you must do something that <u>only</u> you have done. Then, and only then can you take pride in your creation. Then and only then are you truly relevant.

And Then the Time Was Gone

08/January/2015 13:04

I was cruising home today, listening to the radio, and a song I recorded way back in the way back when came on. It got a lot of airplay back then.

Whenever I hear it on the radio it always kind of bothers me. Bothers me because I never made a dime from it. Somebody did, but not me. I gained no fame from it either, because I was trying to be all-dark and obscure back then so I used a pseudonym. The guy I recorded it with took the song and the band name and made a bit of a name for himself in the U.K. But, what can you do? I am sure I am not the only one with this tale to tell...

Hearing the song did make me think, however. Think about how we each set a course for ourselves, based upon what we desire. But, most of us never see that dream happen.

So many times when I met people they tell me what path they are on and what they are going to achieve. Years later they are still working at the same go-nowhere job and/or have given up on their dreams. I think this is very sad.

Some, due to love, throw it all away... I have known several people who were actually on the path to achieving their end-goal but then they met someone, ran away with that person, and lost all chance of obtaining what they truly desired. In some cases I have bumped into these people years later and they each tell the same story of love-gone-bad, (as it generally tends to do), and now all they are is full of regret.

It is like in high school... There, everyone has the dream for what they are to become. As I look back, I feel that I was very blessed to have been able to go to high school and spend my free time actualizing the next step of my reality. Whereas many of my contemporaries had to get a job while in high school, I did not. Which I am (now) very thankful for as most of the people who did get a job, never finished high school.

Me, I went to school but I would also meet with prominent yogis and spiritual teachers. I would go to the Sufi Dances on Monday night. First, I studied and then later taught yoga. The martial arts, and my teaching of them, were always there, of course. But, these were never a job. They were a lifestyle and a means for me to define who I was later to become. You can't teach until you have studied...

On the weekends my friend Saturday Jim and I would head out to our friend's house in the valley and play music, hike in the local mountains, and get shit-faced drunk. We would show up to school on Monday morning wearing the same clothing that we left Hollywood with on Friday night. As most of my friends we older, if they invited me to San Francisco, Santa Cruz, Yosemite, or up to the nude hot springs in the mountains, I was there.

All of this set the stage for the dichotomy my life was to become and I loved it. I was allowed to take my early years and define me.

But, this is the thing... At the end of the day all we are left with is all we are left with. What we are left with is what we have done. What we have done is defined by what opportunities we had and then the choices we made within those opportunities.

Most people set about to do something with their life, but most fail. Some fail because they never really try. Some fail because they quit. Some fail because of the choices that they make. Some fail because life will not allow it. Some fail because they set a gateway of negativity in front of themselves by what they have said about other people and what they have done to other people. Some fail because the dream is simply impossible.

On the other side of the coin, those who succeed are blessed by luck, good karma, destiny, and their own focused dedication.

But, the reality is, you cannot become something you were not destine to become, no matter how hard you try. You can only be what you can only be.

To this end, we must each do what we do, no matter where we find ourselves in life. We must each focus on and move towards our dream. As long as you do not harm anybody else in the doing, then there is nothing wrong with the trying.

But remember, just like the song I mentioned at the beginning of this piece, just because you achieve something does not mean that it will be the answer to all of your dreams.

In fact, your achieving something may cause you as much frustration as satisfaction.

 Life is a strange mess...

Don't Fuck With Religion

08/January/2015 07:59

There is a number of reasons why I am not a fan of religion. Perhaps the biggest one is the fact that people kill each other over it like what happened yesterday in Paris.

Now, some may say that the magazine staff that was attack asked for it, as they were openly poking fun at a religious deity. Others would say that was their right to say and portray anything that they want. But, we currently live in a very volatile time and people look for a reason to lash out. Yeah, the gunmen played the bully mentality. They went in with assault rifles and wiped out unarmed people. But, in their minds I am sure they believed it was the magazine that was committing the sin and as the magazine would not stop doing what they were doing they believed they had no other options. So, who ultimately is to blame? That will forever remain the question throughout all aspects of life.

If you do, you will be done to. That is a fact.

People who are religious are very religious. This is true no matter what religion a person practices. The Middle East has been aflame forever. It is just that more recently the zealot nature of religion has spread across the globe.

The fact of the matter is there are a lot of crazy people out there. Look at the people who assassinated JFK, MLK, and John Lennon or the people who tried to kill Ronald Reagan, Larry Flynt, or George Harrison. Then there are those like the Charlie Manson crew who used a song as a motivator to unleash havoc and kill people. They're all fucking crazy! Add religion to that insanity and it turns into a real mess.

What I do not understand is why religious people do not ask themselves one very probing question, *"If god and his deities are truly omnipresent and all-powerful why would they even care what someone is saying about them?"*

It is man that gets upset about god and religion, not god. Man wants to find a reason to prove he is more powerful than someone or something else, not god. Man does stuff like kill people, not god.

If you are religious stop lying to yourself about why you are doing something. You are not doing it for the truth and the honor of god; you are doing it for yourself.

I Want To Give You Some Money

07/January/2015 08:12

I received a rather amusing email shortly before Christmas. Somebody was contacting me to tell me that they loved what I did and wanted to give me some money. Okay...

As I always semi-jokingly state, *"Everybody always wants something from me but nobody ever gives me anything."* Whether it's people wanting to be in my films, wanting me to give them my films, books, music, or art, people wanting me to teach them how to do something, or people just wanting to suck my energy, I always seem to meet people like that – people who want to take but who do not want to give.

I think we all make our deals with the devil very early in life and whether knowingly or not at the time we set the course for our life in motion. Mine is to give. Others are to take. And, that's okay with me. I guess it's the deal I made. I don't know?

But life and money is a funny thing. We all need money to survive. Thus, we all need to find a way to make money to survive.

Over the years I have seen so many people move here to L.A. to make it. As L.A. seems to be one of those magnates. Whether it was to make it as an actor, filmmaker, musician, or whatever – people hear the stories, think that they've got what it takes, and come here. But, most fail. Most end up broke and have to return to their families. L.A. is one of the prime examples of where people come to succeed but end up broke and nowhere.

But, it is not only people who come here seeking illusive success. One of my longtime friends, now in fifties, kind of got messed around by a woman, lost his job, so he and his teenage son had to move back in with his mother and her husband. A sad reality. But, at least he has a mother and a family.

This is the thing, money controls everything. So, we all need to make it. When we don't, we're screwed.

We can get paid for what we do, our labor. That is the most common way to make money. We can get paid for what we create. But now, in this day and age, I can tell you from personal experience, people rob you blind in the world of cyberspace. They do it by what they take for free, that is not theirs to take, they do it by what they say, and they do it without a second thought; they care not about their karma. Not right, but reality. So, getting paid in the today of today is sketchy at best.

But still, at the end of the day, we all need money. So, when someone offers to give it to us, whether that is via a job offer or like the person in the email said to me, they loved what I did and simply wanted to give it to me, it catches our attention. But, I guess the ultimate reality of reality comes down to who and what we are. I just have never been a good gift receiver, so though the email caught my attention, I did not respond. But, you can send me the money if you really want to. :-)

DSLR Cinematography

06/January/2015 08:11

Over the past several years many people have taken to using their DSLR cameras to film their independent films and music videos. The reason for this is twofold: One, the cameras are generally much cheaper to buy than a good camera that is actually designed to shoot live action video. Two, due to the fact that you can easily change the lenses on these cameras they give the would-be filmmaker varying cinematic options. Though, on a basic level, these cameras do provide a fairly good video image, there are also several problems with using them as a tool to film a competent movie.

The initial problem that arises with using a DSLR, as a filmmaking tool, comes from the way in which it focuses. Whereas the focusing mechanism in a video camera is designed to find, focus, and capture a moving image, this is not the case with a DSLR. DSLR focusing is designed to capture a still image, (as they are actually designed as a still frame camera). To this end, if you are going to use your DSLR camera to film a movie you really need to work with lock-off shots. Meaning, set up a tripod, get your actors in place, and then let them do their stuff with little or no spherical or to-and-fro movement. If you work within a standardized lock-off shot format then your DSLR can capture a nice image.

For me, personally, I find the lock-off shot very boring. I like visual movement. To this end, whenever I use one of my DSLR cameras to film people, I very precisely lock the focus and keep the subject(s) at a static and standardized distance. From this, the figures appear to have movement while keeping them in focus and preventing the camera from attempting to find focus.

The second problem with using a DSLR camera, as a filmmaking tool, comes from its capability to record sound. Almost every digital camera from the point and shoots up to the high end DSLRs now have built-in microphones. The problem is, these microphones are terrible. They produce horrible sound. In controlled internal situations you can get okay audio, but never good. If you go outside, forget about it.

Most higher-end DSLRs do have an external microphone input. If you are going to shoot with a DSLR get a high-end mic and use it! This being said, the way a DSLR processes sound is also not as good as the way a camera designed to shoot video does.

Now, I'm not going to go into a long discourse about sound here. If you want to read the everything about the superiority of the XLR microphones and the appropriate microphones and cables that drive them you can read my book *Zen Filmmaking* or find information online. I will say, high-end mics are not designed to be feed into a camera through a mini plug, as the DSLR provides. Your sound will be altered. It will be much better than using the on-board mic but it will be altered. So, expect that.

On the other side of the issue there are some microphones that are designed to mount on a DSLR camera and provide you with superior sound. Yes, they do give you better sound. But again, they are not a professional XLR microphone, driven through an XLR port, so you must keep that in mind.

Personally, whenever I use a DSLR, as a filmmaking tool, I use it only to capture a visual image. I never expect the sound to be usable.

The fact is, the DSLR is, no doubt, going to continue to be used in filmmaking situations. But, if you use one, you must keep in mind that though they can capture video, that is not what they are designed to do. It is an after thought. If you plan to shoot a visually stimulating film, the best thing to do is to actually go with a camera that is designed to shoot video. The best cameras for that purpose have always been the ones created by Sony. Though Canon is a big player in the market, their cameras forever have underlying issues. Sony is a much better product.

At the end of the day, if you want to be a filmmaker, I always say, get out there and do it. Make your movie in the best way (any way) you can. So, if you have a DSLR to work with, do it. Even if you just have a point and shoot or your phone – if you want to film visual images, use whatever you have.

This being said, it is important to keep in mind that every medium has its limitations. Work with what you have but understand the limitations.

Love it to Death

05/January/2015 13:10

    I took an AM drive across the inner city today, from the end of Crenshaw Blvd. to the beginning of Crenshaw Blvd. Had my teeth cleaned by this sweet and cute denial hygienist -- my favorite denial hygienist ever. We always try to talk about life, travel, and family but it is hard to do when someone is cleaning your teeth. :-)

    Obviously, she works at my dentist's office. Curious fact; my dentist was born the same day of the same year as me. Interesting... He took over for my first and original dentist who died many years ago. As a child and as a teenager I remember how that dentist used to sit and smoke while working on my teeth. Again, interesting... Just one of those illustrations of how life and life situations have all changed. A point and place in history. But, this is all totally off topic...

    After the dentist, I hit over to one of my favorite hangs outs, *The Original Farmers Market* to get my waffle on. I ordered what I always have: *Number 23, Waffle Versailles* with fresh strawberries and a load of whip crème, butter, and syrup and a latte on the side – non-fat, of course.

    As I sat there I saw this truly interesting young Italian girl. (I know she was Italian because she spoke Italian). As she walked up to the counter to order, I saw she rocked these 80s style baggy, day-glow workout pants and an YST, *(Yves Saint Laurent),* bright red purse. When she got her Waffle Sorbonne, which is a waffle with bananas and chocolate syrup and was walking to her table there was this look of overwhelming joy and anticipation beaming from her eyes. It was really breathtaking. It made me realize that though I like the waffles that I eat there, (and I have eaten there for so many years that I cannot even tell you how many waffles I have eaten), I have never experienced that level of overwhelming, in the moment, perfection of truly enjoying what I ate...

    A few days ago, I hit over to this one *Starbucks* that I used to go to all the time, but now I virtually never go there. It was the first one to land in the South Bay back in maybe '91. I used to love it there. I was in the neighborhood so I grabbed my *Grande Nonfat Latte* and sat back to enjoy it. Soon after I sat down this Native American guy walks outside, sits down, and lights up a cigarette. Obviously, a real annoyance. I guess he didn't get the memo that *Starbucks* is a no smoking zone. I was about to say something, but then I looked at him. I could tell he was straight off the res and here (there) he was in the perfect embodiment of *Disneyland:* the big city and *Starbucks.* He had the look of pure joy and satisfaction in his eyes as he sat there drinking a simple coffee and smoking his cigarette. He was in paradise.

Now, I go to *Starbucks* pretty much everyday; sometimes twice. So yeah, I like the place. But, I have never felt what that man was feeling. I could not take anything away from him so I said nothing and just left.

This is an interesting point for all of us to think about. How much of our life, how many times in our life, do we do anything that provides us with that much purpose, passion, and overwhelming joy? The thing is, this is not something that we can decide to do. Sure, we can fake it and pretend that we are all-embodied with impassioned, in the moment, fulfillment. But, that is just a mind game. It is not reality. The only time that reality is real is when we naturally experience something like these two people did. But, again, how often does that happen?

It would be nice to feel that way all the time, I suppose. But, since we can't, I guess observing those who are experiencing it from time to time will have to do. :-)

Sorry

03/January/2015 18:09

If you are not saying that you are sorry to someone whose life you damaged, you are saying the wrong thing.

If you are not feeling remorse for damaging someone's life, you are feeling the wrong thing.

If you are not attempting to fix the thing you damaged in someone's life, you are doing the wrong thing.

Life is an ongoing course of events set in motion by you.

You are one-hundred present responsible for what you say, what you do, and what happens to the people who are affected by what you say and what you do.

If what you have said or what you have done has hurt anyone, then you are responsible for fixing it.

You said it, you did it, thus you are responsible for it.

No hiding from this fact, lying about this fact, or denying this fact will ever change anything.

You have no right to pass judgment on anyone.

You have no right to do anything to anybody that they do not want you to do.

No matter what your logic, justification, or reasoning, if you hurt people, your life will forever be in chaos.

Say good things. Do good things. Hurt no one. Fix what you have broken. This is the key to expressing a good life.

Future Hope

03/January/2015 10:06

    You can hope that your future will be brighter.
    You can believe that your life will get better someday.
    You may not ever think about the fact that what you say and do today, creates your tomorrow.
    What you do, what you say, how you act towards others, you are responsible for.
    What you do, what you say, how you act towards others sets everything in this life in motion.
    Anger equals anger. Fear equals fear. Lies equal lies. Deception equals deception. Jealousy equals jealousy. Hurt equals hurt. Unconscious, unthinking behavior equals unconscious, unthinking behavior. Truth equals truth. Love equals love.
    What are you doing? What are you saying? What life are you setting in motion?

Why You Are Thinking It

03/January/2015 10:05

Why are you thinking and feeling what you are thinking and feeling?

Are you doing it because that is what you truly think or feel? Or, are you doing it because someone told you to think or feel that way?

Maybe, you hope to impress someone with making them believe that is the way you think and feel?

Thoughts and feelings are the sourcepoint for life. All life is created due to what you think and what you feel.

As your thoughts and feelings are the impetus of all life, what are you going to create? A world were people say and do positive things? Or, a world dominated by criticism, anger, disregard for personal integrity, and negativity?

You create your world. What are you going to invoke and experience?

I Learned My Lesson

31/December/2014 09:36

"I learned my lesson." This is something that someone commonly says when he or she has come to understand that they are doing something wrong and are going to stop. This wrong could be something that they were doing to themselves, like smoking, taking drugs, drinking too much, spending too much money, using their credit card too much, doing something else bad to their body or mind, and so on. It can also mean that a person has realized that they possess a bad trait in their behavior and are hurting themselves and others by behaving in this way. This can be a bad behavior trait such as being rude, unthinking, jealous, deceitful, envious, hateful, mean-spirited, selfish, and so on. This many also mean that an individual has realized that they are doing something wrong to someone else or other people in general and they are going to stop. This behavior trait may have been treating a particular person in a bad manner or doing something that is realized to be wrong on a bigger scale.

Life is a process of realizations. Very few (if any) of us never do anything that is wrong or shortsighted. And, few pass though life without doing something that injures another person.

We could say that at least a person who is trying to change, who makes the statement, "I learned my lesson," can be commended for attempting a change. Yes, but that is not the only part to this equation.

For many, life is a very selfish place. They think about themselves first and other second, if at all. They do what they feel like doing until they can do it no more – until they are forced to not do it any longer. And, everyone else be damned. Who cares? But, once they are forced to stop doing something, it is only then that they make the statement, *"I learned my lesson."*

I believe if we look at the big picture of life, we will all say this is very sad. People should not behave in this manner. People should think about every action they take, look at it through they eyes of other people to see how it affects the grand scheme, and only then do it if no one is injured in the process. But, this is wishful thinking. It is not reality. People do what they do until they are forced to stop.

This leads us to the second part of the equation. Whenever you are doing something that is damaging, either to yourself or someone else, someone or something is being hurt. And, this hurt can take on many forms. Now what? Yes, you may have learned your lesson and stopped doing what you were doing, but what about the damage you left in your wake?

You know, if we look to the big bank financial scam that took place a couple of years ago, there were all of those investment bankers, doing all this stuff. Not only did they wreck the lives of many people but they messed with the global economy, as well. All of this was based in personal greed, making money for themselves. And, this pattern is not only limited to those who participated in that debacle. This type of behavior has gone on forever. Few are ever sent to jail for their actions. But, like I have said forever, even if someone goes to jail for what they have done wrong, how does that fix anything? How does that right or undo what they have done?

Here lays the ultimate question you must ask yourself if you ever reach a point in your life where you state, *"I learned my lesson."* You must then determine, *"How can I fix what I have broken?" "How can I undo any damage that I have done?"* For without that caveat added to your statement, once again all you are doing is something based in a selfish point of view. You are not doing anything to give to the greater good.

Be more than a person that only thinks about him or herself. From this, the whole world gets better.

Environmental Fighting

30/December/2014 08:58

As martial artists we continually train or bodies and our minds to encounter combative situations in the most effective and expedient manner possible. To this end, we must continually reevaluate and refine our training methods to ensure that we will be prepared to defend ourselves no matter where a battle finds us. For this reason, *Environmental Fighting* is one of the best training methods available.

Environmental Fighting finds the martial artist setting up a situation where he or she is in a less than ideal fighting posture and then must effectively defend him or herself from this positioning. Thus, the practitioner develops the natural ability to refine their defensive and offensive methodology to met whatever type of combat they encounter.

In most martial art classes, students train in a very sterile manner. They face off against their training partner and then performed prescribed blocks to specific punches or kicks. Or, they may perform specific hand-techniques designed to defend against a specific grab or hold. Though these are all age-old training methods, if that is the only self-defense training one practices, if they finds themselves in street combat, where no rules apply, they are often left with a less then ideal skillset of what to do against a wildly driven thug.

To begin to work with *Environmental Fighting* you simply need to set up a combat situation and then have your opponent move in towards you with various random attacks. Obviously, in the initial stages of *Environmental Fighting Training*, your opponent is not going to come at you full speed or with full power. But, by simply unleashing an undefined technique in your direction you will be forced to come to understand what defense is most appropriate and effective against that type of assault.

In is essential in *Environmental Fighting Training* to make sure your defensive techniques are realistic to the environment where you find yourself. For example, when I was a young boy, my instructor set up a chair and a small table in the classroom and demonstrated how he could deliver a roundhouse kick to the head of his opponent across the table.

Though this was an early example of *Environment Fighting*, even then I realized that if you were in a crowded restaurant, sending a wide roundhouse kick to the head of your opponent was not going to be an easy feat to perform as you may get hung up on the table next to you or by a guest dining next to you and so on. The point is, though you will obviously be training in *Environmental Fighting* in the dojang, it is essential to be sure to train in a realistic manner.

The dojang environment is a safe and controlled place where you can refine your training skills and make *Environmental Fighting* a part of your overall training régime. To do so, is quite simple. You simply need to place yourself in an unrehearsed, less than ideal position, and then have your training partner come at you with various aggressive techniques. For example, one *Environmental Fighting* technique to work with is to have your back up against the wall where your opponent has pinned you in. From this training position you will learn how to effectively push your opponent back and deliver close-contact strikes to his body that will leave him disabled.

Another ideal training posture work with is to be sitting on the floor when your attacker accosts you. From this position you will learn how to best deal with low kicks that are directed towards your head and body and how to quickly and effectively get up and reposition yourself and then continue through with appropriate self-defense.

Laying face down, like you may be doing at the beach, is another training posture of *Environmental Fighting* to work with. By discovering how to defend yourself from a fully prone position, perhaps the hardest of all positions to effectively emerge from, you will gain invaluable knowledge about true methods of self-defense.

The main thing to keep in mind when working with *Environmental Fighting* is to never let your techniques become stagnate or predetermined, nor should you ever believe that what works for your training partner will work for you. Each situation and each person possess a completely unique set of variables. For this reason, you must never believe that one technique will universally work in all situations. You must forever be willing to immediately change your defensive strategy the moment you come to understand that it will not leave you dominate in any physical combat situation you find yourself in. *Environmental Fighting* is the ideal training method to develop the insight into what truly works and how you can emerge victorious from any confrontation.

The Unexpected Virtue of Ignorance

28/December/2014 09:18

I was watching a screener copy of the film, *Birdman: The Unexpected Virtue of Ignorance* last night. It is nominated for several SAG Awards for which I will have to vote. Good film.

I am not sure how the movie came into being but casting Michael Keaton, who walked away from the role of Batman in his real life, was genius. As that is what the film follows, an actor who once played a superhero and then his career fell away, so he is trying to rekindle it by doing a play on Broadway.

The film really highlights how there are those who feel the only true actors are those on the New York stage and everyone else is not the real deal. That belief is very common throughout the film industry.

Here in L.A., however, there is really no good theatre. The only reason actors do it at all is if they can't get roles in movies or hope to advance their career by taking to the stage, as many agents require that experience listed on the resume. Me, I hate theatre. It is so boring. I really see it, along with karaoke, as one of god's curses to this earth. I love the visual movement and the stimuli of film. And, that is just it... To each there own.

That is one of the ultimate lessons of life: I like this, you like that, and that is that.

The thing is, and this is one of things illustrated in this film, some people try to force what they like and what they believe down the throat of other people and are willing to damn the life of that person in the process. I think we should all learn from this and never follow this practice. We should be true to ourselves and what we believe in but never force or expect others to believe what we believe.

Be silent onto your own truth, so sayeth Scott Shaw. :-)

Enlightenment at the Hands of Evil
27/December/2014 19:34

I forever find it perplexingly interesting how through various life events we are each given the ability to grow in our understanding of Self and of Life. Sometimes, these learning exercises are provided to us via methods we would have preferred not to have ever encountered in the first place. None-the-less, if we allow ourselves to grow from them, we can become a better person – learning what to do and what not to do – how to behave and how not to behave.

A few times in this blog (so far) and more pronounced in *The Scott Shaw Zen Blog 3.5*, I have discussed the damning actions of one of my neighbors. ...How he claims to be some sort of spiritual something and one minute he will be speaking very loudly to the people who will listen to him, telling them how they should live their life, and the next minute he will be screaming, *"Fuck me,"* at the top of his lungs. He should be ashamed of himself. There are few things worse in this world than a person who markets themselves as a proponent of spirituality yet lives a lifestyle that is just the opposite.

Now, we all have, *"Fuck me,"* moments in our life. Certainly, I have had mine. But, I never found it necessary to scream, *"Fuck me! Fuck me! Fuck me! Fuck me and mine,"* over and over again at the top of my lungs, while stomping my feet like this man does. Not when I was teenager, when emotions tend to run hotter, nor as an adult. And, this man is totally grey, so you can guess at his age.

In fact, I actually inadvertently recorded one of his, *"Fuck me,"* rants one time. I was sitting down at my computer to record a joking Christmas message to my advanced martial arts students, two Christmas' ago, and all of a sudden it started, which obviously caused me to stop speaking. Afterwards, I realized it had been recorded.

I have an attorney on retainer. Though nothing like that had ever happened to me before, I decided to talk to him about the matter. So, I took a copy of the recording to his office. After hearing it, my attorney wanted to contact the police, report the guy to the people who had rented him the place, and sue him for one thing or another. But me, being who I am, I didn't let that happen. (My attorney always reminds me that I am his worst client). I just assumed that the neighbor would sooner-or-later realize that no one around him wanted to hear any of his nonsense. I did joking think to do what all those sample artists do and add music to his rant. But, that's not the kind of music I make. So, I did, like I always do in these situations, I left the copy in the hands of my attorney just incase something jumped off farther down the line.

Here, we come to the main point of the main point. If you claim to be a spiritual anything, you must set a higher standard for yourself than to behave in such an unconscious manner that you truly ruin the lives of not only those you purport to teach but those people simply existing around where you find yourself. Now, I am not just saying this about the people that he lectures, but never meets, via the phone line or the web, or however he dishes out his dissertations. But, I am speaking about the people living around him. For if you have damaged the lives of other people, by unthinking behavior, how can you claim to be helping anyone else? If you don't treat average life as sacred, how can you speak of and teach advanced consciousness?

You see, this is the reason why people get so upset when it is found out that a priest molested a young person or when a minister criticizes gays and adulteresses, and then is found out to be doing the same thing himself. If you claim spirituality, you must forever, in all things, represent spirituality. You must be more!

In the Hindu and Buddhist tradition, when people want to leave behind desire and pay for the sins they have committed, they retreat from the world. In the Christian tradition, the true zealot may go to a monastery and pray for forgiveness. But, in this mishmash world of spirituality there is no honor. Thus, there is no payment for the crimes. Most of these people only deny their actions, let alone acknowledge them. They never apologize for them. Certainly, my neighbor has not apologized to me. He continues to do what he does, deceiving people who will listen to him without ever telling them who he truly is. All this is just wrong!

And, it is not like you can report people like this to the *Better Business Bureau* or talk shit about them on Yelp. All you can do is hope that the negative karma they have created will hurry up and catch up with them and get them out of your life.

You know, and this is the thing... I never wanted this. I never asked for it. I never hoped to hear this guy (or anybody else for that matter) loudly spit out regurgitated spiritual wisdom one minute, then the next minute try to pick up on a girl via the phone and then when she turns him down, calling someone else and telling them what a bitch she is. How is that spiritual on any level? But, he dragged me and the other neighbors into his world. Just wrong! It is not spiritual!

...If he was just some loud guy, being a jerk, you would just consider him and asshole. But, when he is claiming spirituality it sets a whole new set of rules and definitions into motion...

I really think I should state something for the record here... Some people have tried to define me as spiritual, but I never claim that. I was initiated into the *Saraswati tradition* of Hinduism via Swami Satchidananda, *the Sufi Order* via Pir Vilayat Inayat Khan, the *Vietnamese Thiền Buddhist tradition* via Thích Thiên-Ân. I received *Shaktipat* and was initiated into *Siddha Yoga* by Swami Muktananda. I was initiated into *Tantra Yoga* by Swami Ahimsananda. I received *Neo-Sannyass* initiation by Bhagwan Shree Rajneesh, (which was an event onto itself), *Sanyass* initiation by Swami Ramanada. I was initiated into *Theravada Buddhism* by Phra Ajaan Sao Sanampakasoon. I received final initiation and became a *Frater* of the *Rosicrucian Order* as well as *The Martinist Order.* I studied with Israel Regardie of *the Golden Dawn* (who amazingly made his living as a chiropractor), among many other teachers of the Eastern and Western traditions. Plus, I was the *Senior Patrol Leader* of my *Boy Scout Troop* before I quit. You know what all that means? It means absolutely nothing! It means, at best, I have the credentials to write some books, some articles, and some discourses like this, but nothing else. I claim nothing! I am just a *down mutha fucka.* Yet, here I am, giving this guy the only fame he will ever know because of him claiming to be a spiritual something, lying and deceiving people, while fucking up the lives of those people living in his vicinity by being a loud mouth and never shutting up.

Sometimes, you have to question, *"Why?"*

And, this is it, this is the point, we are each going to be defined by events and by people who enter our lives. Some of these events and some of the people we welcome. Others, will completely mess up our peace and our existence. And, if they are doing this while claiming to be a spiritual conduit, we can only question, *"What is god thinking? And, why does he let this type of blasphemy go on?"*

But... This is life. We are each going to meet our own worst demons. We can hate it and become angry with them or we can learn from what they are doing wrong and gain enlightenment from their evil.

This is not the ideal way towards enlightenment but sometimes it is all we have.

Salvation Mountain

27/December/2014 08:58

Amazingly, the documentary I shot about *Salvation Mountain* and its creator Leonard Knight, fourteen years ago, is finally going to be released early in 2015.

I hadn't been there for a few years so I thought I would take a look and see what is going on. Sadly, it has become an unappreciative tourist stop with people stomping all over everything; complete with a few men taking people on walking tours, claiming to have known Leonard and misstating his ideologies and facts about his life. And, charging to do it! Sad!

Leonard moved away from the site a couple of years ago. With his death, earlier this year, I believe that unless someone else steps in and takes over the upkeep and manages what people are doing to the site, the structures on *Salvation Mountain*, will soon fall away.

Waiting for Santa to Arrive

25/December/2014 01:00

So, with the typical Christmas Eve festivities behind me, I kick back to watch the TV screen...

Now, I must say, and this is kind of weird for me to say, as I am not at all about the, *"I am that."* But, and/or, in any case, as I am member of SAG/Aftra, and the SAG/Aftra Awards Nomination Committee, I am sent films before they are ever released to the public. So, I get see a lot of movies before they are seen by the whole and/or if the general public ever sees them at all. In many ways, I find this weird. It makes me feel like one of those meaningless reviewers who tries to make a name for themselves by talking about other people's movies. As that is not who I am, on any level... But, as stated, as I am a member of SAG/Aftra, and the SAG/Aftra Awards Nomination Committee, they send these films to me anyway.

Okay... Backstory done. I started watching a couple of projects. Projects that I may have to vote on the future... I just couldn't do it. This is Christmas Eve. So, I turned my attention to other things...

I was flipping channels and I came upon the 1977 release, *The Grateful Dead Movie.*

Now, before I get into the all and the everything about the rest of what I will say, I must state, I was never a big fan of *The Grateful Dead.* Sure, they have a couple of songs that I liked, Friend of the Devil, Saint Stephen, and... But, I never really got it. In my youth, I had gone to a couple of *Grateful Dead* concerts and the people would all be dancing around hippie style. But, I would just sit there and wonder, *"Why?"* It was like a weird breed of country music, not rock. In fact, in 1976, just after graduating from *Hollywood High School,* I was living in Yosemite. I had my Fender 12-String guitar, a cool group of friends, and we would spend our days playing music, singing, hiking, rock climbing, getting high, and making love. One day there came the rumor that *The Grateful Dead* were to play in *Golden Gate Park.* So me, bored with the scene, I packed up. I left my friend Spinky (who had the greatest fro ever) behind to hang in the vastness of Yosemite. He didn't want to go. Me, I got into my 1974 Chevy Vega, and drove to the city while listening to tapes of *Alan Watts, Ram Dass, Neil Young,* and *The Doors.* I got there in the evening, found a place to park, not far from the where the concert was rumored to be, and slept in the backseat of my car.

Day next, I did what I did in the AM. I got chocolate milk and a yogurt in *The Haight* and walked around the panhandle section of *Golden Gate Park,* where the concert was to be held. There were a lot of people who had heard the same thing as I. They were all wondering around, wondering where and when it was going to happen. Time went on and nothing. Jerry Garcia had apparently bailed. Probably too high from the junk he was addicted to. Or, maybe it was all just a lie. Me, I had a car. Most did not. I wanted to drive over to Jerry's house, across The Bay, and say. *"What's up?"* But, what would that have equaled?

What did happen, however, was while I was in the park that day, I met this very special lady. She, like I, was in the park, waiting for the concert. She, not like I, was a big fan of *The Dead.* But, it did not happen. Post our figuring out that *The Dead* were not going to play, my suggestion to her and her friend was to go back to Yosemite with me. Which we eventually did…

Okay… That was then. Me, I eventually had other things to do like go to India. She went back to New York. Many, many years later she contacted me via the internet. We, were like forty something years old by that point in time. She was now living in San Francisco. Living in *The Haight,* not far from where we first met. We hooked up. We did what we did. Then, I hit back to L.A.; my home.

…After our moment, she contacted me on every birthday. The last time I spoke with her was on my birthday. I was in SF, she was in SF, but I was with someone else, so meeting would have just been weird. During that conversation she told me she had cancer. That was the last time I ever heard from her; years ago…

Now, every birthday, I expect her to call. A call that never comes. I guess she moved onto the next life?

And, this is the thing about life. For each of us, it is here and then it is gone. We do what we do; interact with whom we interact with, but then, all that is left in the memories. …The memories of those who survive the other. Not right, for sure. But, this is life.

In 1977, I saw *The Grateful Dead Movie* in the theater. That was then. What it is now, is a total illustration of a time and a place.

As mentioned, in the beginning of this discourse, I get to see a lot of films. Films that, in some cases, other people will never see. The one thing that I can tell you is that, films that portray the seventies always get it wrong. If you want to see what people looked like and acted like in the 1970s, see the film, *The Grateful Dead Movie*.

I Did It Because…

24/December/2014 08:50

Everybody has a reason for doing what he or she did. That reason may be an excuse. That reason may be a justification. That reason may be a self-believed fact. But, a reason is never the truth. A reason is only a reason.

I did it because I was young. I did it because I was stupid. I did it because I was angry. I did it because I was horny. I did it because I was jealous. I did it because I was envious. I did it because I was hurt. I did it because I was hungry. I did it because I was broke. I did it because I was drunk. I did it because I was in love. I did it because I wasn't thinking. I did it because I was only thinking about myself. I did it because I didn't know any better. I did it because I didn't care. I did because I was wrong.

These statements, and many more, all define the, *"I did it because,"* mentality.

In life, we all do the things that we do. Some of these things are good, wholesome, and helpful. Some of these things are just the opposite; they are hurtful, desireful, and damaging. But, it is we who do them. Once done, we can claim all kinds of misplaced logic and excuses to justify our actions. But, it is all meaningless words because the ultimate truth is what was done is what was done.

This is why if you want your life to be more than simply a long list of excuses and emotional or desire-filled episodes you must take control of your mind, and never let your lower-self control what you do. For where is all regret born. It is born from actions taken by the lower-self.

No one is perfect. We have all done things that we regret. We have all done things that other people make us regret. But, if you choose to live your life consciously, you will not want to be defined by a long list of, I did it because…

Consciously become more.

Wanting To Be More

23/December/2014 16:22

In my last couple of blogs I have written about people that want to be something more. More, than what they actually are.

The fact of the matter is, we all want to be something more. No matter how successful we are, everyone wishes that they had more and were more. Virtually no one but the true monk is ever satisfied with being less or nothing: no-thing.

But, what comes into play in this fact is how we individually address the complex issue of become more. Some people consciously work towards their desired end goal. They do this by orchestrating a focused, precisely devised game plan. They do it in a manner that helps them grow, while damaging no one's life in the process. This is the ideal way to achieve any desired end goal.

Other people, however, as discussed in the previous two blogs, lie about who and what they are and charge forward leaving devastation in their wake. This is obviously not the right way to achieve anything, for this path leaves the person far too burdened with the lingering distaste of others and an abundance of negative karma. So much so, that they will never be able to rise to the level of success they hope to achieve. Thus, they become damned by their own actions.

All of the people that lie about who they are or who they were are not necessarily bad people, however. For example, I know this one man who when I first met him, twenty-five years ago or so, he used to tell the story about how he was a civilian contractor in Asia. As time has gone on, however, his story and the lie attached to it has grown and grown. First he began by stating that he was actually not a contractor but was in the CIA. Then his story expanded from him working in one country onto rescuing political prisoners in several other countries. One time I asked him what was the name of the military group he was attached to. *"We were known as the A-Team,"* he proclaimed. With this, it was hard not to laugh, as we all know about the TV show and the movie with this title. But, I held it in.

Now, this guy is not a bad person. And, the simple accomplishments he has achieved; i.e. having a good career, being married, and raising a successful son should be enough. But, to some, this man included, they want the glory and the admiration. Thus, the lie is given birth to.

As I also discuss frequently, we are so bombarded by the greatness of others: whether they are *Movie Stars, Music Stars, Reality TV stars,* or the actual *Superheroes* we see on film, that this is what becomes the desired norm. We want to be more! We want to be great! We want to have done something great! We want everyone to love us!

The fact is, there is no cure for any of this. The only cure is to not possess the desire to be something more than you already are. Though that seems very logical, it is not the mindset that most people possess. Thus, all of the nonsenses of lying, deceiving, and hurting other people, in the process of gaining what you want, is given birth to.

I can say, let go of all of your desires and you will be free, but you probably won't listen. Therefore, the only thing you can do on your road to accomplishment is to be true to who and what you actually are at each stage of your evolution. Don't lie about yourself. Next, as you consciously progress towards your goals, always think about others first – take others into consideration first and never hurt or damage the life of anyone in your quest for greatness. From this, people will admire your tenacity and not quiver at what is the next lie you will tell or the next destructive action you will take.

Really... Being less is being more.

Lost in Their Own Lie

22/December/2014 20:21

Kind of building on my previous blog, I forever find it curious how people become lost in their own lie. I believe that this is most probably based upon the fact that they have achieved very little with their life and hope to make someone else believe that they are something more than they actually are. From making someone believe their lie, they may hope that their myth will grow. But, if it is born in a lie, a lie is all that it will ever be. And, if a person is not honest at the outset of any relationship, that relationship is doomed as it is forever defined by the lie.

When people are young and they are seeking out a mate they may stretch the truth to make themselves seem like something more. That is not necessarily right, but it is understandable. As people get older, however, that style of behavior usually falls away. But, it some cases it does not.

Again, we go back to the point of the premise that is; if a person is something, if they have actually achieved something, they would not need to boast and/or alter the truth, and they would not need to tell people about who and what they believe themselves to be, because people would already know. But, from the desire to be seen as something more, whether consciously or not, the deceitful person continues to tell the same lie over and over and over again. If you have to listen to it, that lie becomes very trying. And, a lie never becomes the truth. Perhaps the most damming factor of all of this is that a person who behaves in this fashion may even believe their own lie.

I am forever confounded when I encounter people who are so lost in seeking approval that they not only lie to achieve it but they do not think about the consequences of deceiving other people. The fact is, whether people call themselves saint or sinner, considered themselves spiritual or not, few deceivers ever possess the ability to step outside of themselves and actually make a personal change. What they most commonly do is pretend to change or fool themselves into believing that they have changed and then return right back to their same patterns of behavior based upon boasting, untruths, or altered truths.

In times gone past, when someone discovered that they were deceived or damaged by the ongoing lying behavior of a person they would go about getting revenge. Whether that be kicking their ass, naming them and telling the world they are a liar, and presenting proof of that fact, or whatever... But now, everyone has become so politically correct that you can't just go up and punch somebodies lights out. Mostly, because they are so weak as an individual, based in their lies, that all they would do is go and cry to the police or somebody like that.

The truth is, something is lost in this modern society as it is propagated that we should all be nice and forgiving. Though this is the case, by doing this, the sinner never pays for their sins and they continue their pattern of destructive behavior.

Though I have written for many years about ways to dodge the negative impact of negative people: be it mental or physical, it is really much more of a pure science to simply make someone pay for their crime, *mano-a-mano*. But, as stated, most liars are too weak. That's why they are a liar. So, the person who is affected by the lie, on whatever level, is left to chart new ways of payback.

Certainly, we will all immediately leave the company of a liar once we know them for what they are. In some cases, however, it is not that easy. We are stuck by various circumstances and have to continue to listen to their lies. Then, all that is left is the damage the individual has unleash upon us. The thing to keep in mind is though their words and actions may have damaged your life, these same words and actions will obviously set the pattern for the rest of their life. Which, because of what they have done is based in a negative action, will ultimately come to destroy them. But, that may be sometime in the future, not here in the now.

We are each defined by what we do and whom we do it to. Life is defined by interpersonal relationships. If we are lost in a distorted view of self, then the thought of and for other people rarely comes to mind. From this, all that there is, is the thought of self and achieving whatever desire is desired. There is no other way to say it but this is simply wrong. It is the wrong way to behave towards other people and it is the wrong way to interact with life, for all it will ultimately do is come to damn the life of the person who behaves in this manner.

    I would say, make the sinner pay. But, the misery they have unleashed in their own life by lying to, deceiving, and damaging the lives of others will be their ultimate downfall. So, you really don't have to do anything. What goes around comes around and those who damage the life of others by unconscious deceitful actions will find their own life ultimately disintegrating into shambles.

Beauty is in the Eye of the Beholder
22/December/2014 14:19

So, I was having a latte (non-fat, of course) and a bagel at my local Starbucks this morning. I was sitting outside, studying the sea, as I like to do. Behind me, a conversation began taking place. There were two people involved: one woman, one man. What caught my attention was how loud, sure of himself, and driven the male participant was. He stated, *"I think I'm a pretty good looking guy. I know this because whenever I talk to other guys they all seem a little jealous."* Okay...

Now, this conversation went on for a quite a while. In fact, it went on for the whole time I was sitting there. I won't bore you with reciting all of the words, but the subject never changed.

When I got up to leave, I expected to turn around and see one of those really good-looking guys. You know: tall, dark, and hansom, a total male model. What I found, however, was a chubby Asian male with bad skin. This whole situation and the discussion that had taken place made me smile.

I believe, that life is our best teacher. Forget the scriptures. If we simply look and listen to what is going on around us, we can truly come to understand the best way to behave and interact in life.

Now, I am sure if a shrink talked to this guy there may be all kinds of interwoven psychological issues going on. But, that doesn't even matter – at least to the learning curve of life. Because we are each surrounded by an untold number of people(s) everywhere we go. Some of them are nice, some are rude and unthinking, and some are just plain stupid. From each of them we can learn how we should and/or should not behave. In very-specific cases, like the previously described situation; here we are presented with an advanced course in what we sound like if we carry on an ego-based conversation with another person as this man did.

Put away the ego, it just makes you sound stupid. Put away trying to tell the world who and what you think you are – because if you are that, you don't have to tell anyone, as they will already know. Stop trying to guide people with whatever bullshit knowledge you think you know, because all that happens from interacting with people in this fashion is that you become the focus of people's distaste and the butt of everyone's joke.

Shut up and BE. It is so much better for everyone concerned.

Movies You Will Never See

21/December/2014 09:12

I just read a very interesting article about films that were pulled from distribution or never released. Some of them were very big dollar productions.

With all that is going on with the debacle of the film, *The Interview*... And, I understand all sides of the issue. Sony (a Japanese company) got hacked. North Korea is pissed and they have nukes and are very close to Japan. And, the distributors, at least at this moment, pulled back from its distribution. So, there was no way for Sony to get the film out there. In the process of all this, a lot of people were hurt, however. So, who is ultimately to blame? I don't know? As everyone in the film game is a participant and a player. So??? I will just leave that question to the annals of karma...

Back here in reality, there are a lot of reasons why films are not released. The biggest one being, they turned out bad and the main creators of them would not let the film get out there. Back in the day, the name Alan Smithee was use by filmmakers who had made a film and ultimately didn't like its outcome. As too much money had gone into it to simply bury it, the creators, to hide from all the shame of it, used this pseudonym.

There's a great group of people who do a project called, *The Smithee Awards.* They track down, screen, and provided awards to the best of the worst. Some of my films have made it. Thanks guys!!!

But, more to the point... A lot of films are lost to the changing tides of time. Look for the film, *London After Midnight.* Gone... All copies disintegrated to never-never-land with the passing hands of time.

Another causation factor is that a lot of films that were made back in the day, before the age of video and digital, were made at a time when a film was only going to be a film. Thus, they never contracted for the rights to use the music or various other elements of the film when new technologies were born. With no release for the music, and the copyright holder refusing to let the music be used in new media, the film was lost. I know this held up the great film, *Two Lane Blacktop* from being released on video for many years. There are others that you will never see in any new medium.

And, this is just one example. People own the rights to their creations; whether it is the character, the screenplay, the music, you name it. And, this is a very litigious society. Have you ever been sued? It is not fun nor is it cheap. So, people wisely choose to not release a product, that they do not own the rights to, over getting sued and losing – which is what happens if you don't own the rights...

I realize that in this digital age people believe that they can grab anything and do whatever they want with it. Of course, this involves grabbing somebody else's something... And, this is the key to the equation. You don't care if it's not yours... If it is yours, you may have a very different ideology. But, this is life...

I too have had films lost to never-never-land. The main one being, *Lingerie Kickboxer.* Done, but never seen. And, that's the thing when you collaborate with other people; each has their own ideas. Don Jackson and I were all-good with the film, our partners wanted a few high-budget changes, that we never got around to making. So... I think it's a great film and a perfect example of true *Zen Filmmaking* but you will probably never see it. Of course, if you wanted to pay me a lot of money I may go and take it out of my film vault at Paramount and set up a private screening for you. :-)

And, this is the thing, simply because you cannot see a specific film as you may want to see it: via video tape, DVD, or streaming, does not mean that it is not out there somewhere and with the right incentive you may view it.

On the other side of the issue, there are tons-and-tons of films that get started and are never finished. Then, there are the finished products that the filmmaker doesn't know what to do with them so they are lost to the viewing eye and never seen. I know several films and filmmakers who have followed this path even thought they had made a really good movie.

So, I guess it all gets back to the Zen of life. If a tree falls in the forest and there is no one there to hear it, does it make a sound at all? Or, if you heard it fall once what happens if it never falls again?

Studying the Subtleties

19/December/2014 08:22

Rather amusingly, I received an email today from a guy who has written a long review about the Zen Film, *Max Hell Frog Warrior*. For some reason he wanted me to read it before it was published; though the review is already on its way to press. Every now and then people do this. Why, I don't really know?

It amazes me, but we made *Max Hell* almost twenty years ago, yet it is still receiving press. I guess we did something right. But, that is not really the point...

The point being, and this is something I see so often with film reviewers, is that they do not study the subtleties of a film as they write their reviews – long or otherwise. And, this is true whether they like the film or not. From a filmmaker's standpoint, I can tell you that all of my Zen Films are full of subtleties: from the dialogue, to where the scenes are shot, onto the camera movement, the set, the set decorations, the lighting, the music, the editing, and beyond. You may need to look for them (as that is the point of subtleties) but they are everywhere. But, reviewers oftentimes overlook this fact.

For example, in *Max Hell Frog Warrior* AKA *Toad Warrior* many reviewers (as did this man) mention the fact that we return to one scene several times. That scene is a Kurosawa influenced moment where my character is on a ridge and the sun has left the sky. My character and my opponent charge at each other with samurai swords in silhouette. It's a beautiful scene. We used this scene several times as a moment of transition between various other scenes in the film. What most everyone fails to take note of, however, is that it is not simply a one-take scene. We shot that scene several times. Thus, what you see in the finished film, if you care enough to study it, is that there are different versions of that scene used for different transitional moment. Thus, equaling filmmaking subtlety.

For me, I don't care if someone bags my films or not. (Though this reviewer wrote a fairly fair appraisal). We all like what we like and don't like what we don't like. What makes me have a less than ideal attitude about some reviewers, however, is that they miss some of the most elemental moments of a film, as they are watching the whole and not studying the intricacies.

And, I believe this goes to life, as well. Most people do not study the subtleties. They plow through any new environment, situation, life experience, or work of art they may encounter with their mind already made up, doing and saying what they have forever done. They are who they are! Their mind is made up! And, the world be damned! But, this is not a good way to live life. Because by behaving in this manner you miss so much of the elemental magic that is available if you step beyond yourself and your preconceived notions and take the time to experience each thing you encounter as new and whole – not simply as something you believe you have the right to pass judgment upon.

I believe that everywhere you go, everything you do, the first thing you need to do is stop, listen, see, and embrace the wholeness of the environment or the work of art. Let it define itself. From this, you will have allowed yourself to take note of and embrace the subtleties. And, this is where the magic is born.

The ultimate truth about life is that you are not in control of anything. At best you are simply a conscious participant. Seek to know the subtleties. Then all life becomes MORE.

Send 'em to India

18/December/2014 08:09

I was in HB (Surf City) yesterday, picking up some props for my next film. I saw this guy walking down the street. He had these magnificent dread locks and a long beard. The thing was, his clothes were in tatters. He was obviously homeless.

The thing is about being homeless, there is virtually no way back. Unless someone takes you in, cleans you up, gives you a place to live so you can get a job or whatever, your life is done. Done... At least here in the States.

Like I have long said, here a person is a homeless bum but in India they are a holy man.

I mean looking at this guy that is exactly what I thought. His dread, his beard, his whole demeanor, he had obviously been living that lifestyle for a long time. If he were in India, people would be feeding him and touching his feet in order to gain his blessings. But here, these people have no chance. There, they could be not only be well taken care of but respected.

Culture and religious understandings; it's a weird thing...

Anyway, if you want to help the homeless, why not put them on a plane to Delhi or Mumbai. That's all you would have to do. From there all they would have to do is walk out into the society and be who they are. Their homeless status would make them a sadhu; thus they would instantly become an embodiment of holiness.

But, the question remains, (with this previous example as an illustration), who or what truly is holy?

Feed Your Brain

17/December/2014 08:45

You are what you eat, as the old saying goes. This is true of your body but it is also true of your mind.

What you feed into your brain is what defines how you act, react, and interact with the world.

In this modern age people are deluged with fictional stimuli. We watch TV, we go to the movies, we play video games. Each of these creations program our mind. The more we see a specific type of film creation or play a particular type of video game the more our brains become programmed by them.

Think about this, have you ever seen a really brutal horror film, where really bad things happen to people? Sure, it is just a film but what it does is create a state of mind, in your mind, which leaves an imprint and from this you are left thinking about the negative visuals that took place in that film. This is the same with TV shows where your mind starts to question why did this happen and/or that should have happened. Yes, it is fantasy, but these creations have the ability to control your mind to the degree that you are left pondering a fictional reality.

Video games, as we all know, can be very violent visualscapes where the players go around killing other players and fighting for survival. Though many people like these games, there is no relaxation provided by them, only adrenalized stimuli. Thus, the heart rate and blood pressure rise and the mental space of the players are left with thoughts of negative actions.

We are all surrounded by these various types of pastimes in this modern life. And, most of us partake of them to one degree or the other. Most of us can separate the fiction from the reality. Some people, however, cannot and from this negative life actions and/or worsening psychological conditions are given birth to.

The fact of the matter is, even those of us who can separate the fiction from reality, presented by the so-called forms of entertainment, are, none-the-less, mentally influenced by their intake. Those of us who do partake are shaped by the images presented to our brain. Think about this, when you think of something really scary and negative does your mind not go to a similar situation you saw in a horror films? When you hear about something really bad having happened to a person on the news does your mind not chart to a scene you saw in a film or on TV?

You are what you eat.

The thing about life, and this is something that many people forget, is that we personally have the power to control our own brain and our own thought patterns. This is one of the things that the science of meditation teaches us, how to take control over our thinking minds.

Most people simply pass through life dominated by whatever their brain is thinking and whatever emotion they are feeling. It doesn't have to be like that! You can make a choice to take control!

The process of personal mental control is really pretty easy. First of all, choose what you feed into your brain. Then, decided what you will or will not think about. When weird or negative thoughts come to mind, feed by what you previously ingested, stop them. You can do it. You simply have to focus and then consciously redirect your mind to a more positive mental place.

Stop eating mental junk food. From this, you and the world becomes a much better place. And, moreover, take control of your mind. It is your mind, it is your thoughts, you do have the ability to control them.

Lady in the Rain

16/December/2014 14:54

It was a rainy day in L.A. A rainy day that tuned into a rainy night. Wait! I can't use that. That's the opening passage to my book, *Junk: The Backstreets of Bangkok.*

Anyway… It was rainy day in L.A. today. I was driving down the street listening to a CD by *Dirty Vega* on the stereo. It was a perfect moment for me. I love driving in the rain, listening to great music.

The rain began to really come down. Over on the sidewalk I noticed a lady walking. My first thought was, she must be getting drenched.

This has probably happened to most of us at one time or another. We are out and about and it starts to rain and we have no rain jacket or umbrella with us. I know it has happened to me more times than I can count in places like Bangkok where the sky instantly opens up and pours out a deluge.

Many times, when I see someone like the aforementioned girl in that predicament, I offer them a ride or give them my umbrella. But, I noticed that she had an umbrella.

There she was, walking down the street in the pouring rain, her large umbrella rolled up, not being used.

I totally understood…

Be More

16/December/2014 09:53

I was watching the series finale of the HBO show, *The Newsroom,* on Sunday. I never thought it was a super-duper show, but it did have its moments and it was something to watch. And, they did mention *Max Hell* in season one, *"Thanks!!!"*

To go into the storyline of the final season would be way too wordy, but, in brief, the guy who was in charge of the internet division of the newsroom went into hiding for most of the season. While he was away the internet division was taken over by these geeks who had just trashed the purpose of the website's design and had filled it with a TMZ style of meaningless internet babble. When the character returned and took the site back over, he told the staff, *"I am embarrassed,"* in regard to what they had done.

Have you ever been embarrassed by what someone has done to what you were closely link to? Have you ever been embarrassed when you wake up to find that you have done something really stupid? Have you tried to cover up, run away from, or lie about your actions? I imagine we all have experienced all of the above, at one point or another in our lives.

The thing is, fun is fun. We all like to have fun. The internet is a great place for mind-numbing fun: *www: the World Wide Waste of time.* But, fun at whose expense is the question?

I just now noticed on the homepage of yahoo a list of, what they claim is, the ten worst actors on TV series. The people they listed are all very successful and they are not bad actors at all. I know, because I have worked with a lot of bad actors. Myself included. :-)

But, it comes down to one thing, what is the point of trashing people? And, who is the person doing the trashing? Who are they? Are they anywhere near as successful as the person(s) they are trashing? No, they are not. But, because they can say anything that they want, about anybody that they want, and not suffer any consequences, that is exactly what they do – just like on TMZ and the fictional site on, *The Newsroom.*

I believe we really need to look into this process and study our own being and how we react to the world. Sure, we all have our own opinion about a person, place, or thing. Some of these opinions are based upon fact but most are based upon speculation founded in internet gibberish. And yeah, I get it. It is sometimes empowering to trash a person or a thing that you don't really like, for whatever reason.... But, you have to remember, all life begins with you. ...You, and what you put out there to the world.

Are you putting good and nice out there? Or, are you putting mean-spirited negativity? ...Some even do it really well, they cloaked their negativity under the guise of humor, parody, or critical evaluation. But, it still equals hurtful negativity, none-the-less.

The answer is very simple to what you should be doing and what you should not be doing in life. How does it feel when you are the focal point of negativity? You may be hiding in your parent's house, typing away at your computer keys, feeling empowered by trashing someone, something, or the whole word, but what does that add up to? All it adds up to is a world defined by misplaced dissociative propaganda.

Do something better with your life. Make a positive difference. And, most important, don't lie to yourself. Don't make excuses for what you are doing and why you are doing it. If you are saying or typing bad things, you are doing bad things. What is the ultimate outcome of that?

Make this world a better place by consciously doing good things.

There and Gone

16/December/2014 08:18

I looked out of my window last night in the early evening. The clouds had gathered in the sky for a rainstorm that was to come. They etched themselves against the sky – the sky meeting the sea. The setting sun was hidden somewhere behind them. But, its illumination was still present.

The entire scene was perfect. The cool air. The hues of blue to grey. The clouds touching the soul of the sea. I studied the shapes of the clouds for a time.

Then, I went back inside for a moment. I had something to complete. A few minutes later I went back to study the perfect scene again. But, it was gone. It had changed. The hidden sun must have left the horizon. Its illumination was no longer there. The clouds and the sea had become much darker. It was still beautiful but it was not the same.

This is an important thing to keep in mind as you pass through life. The perfect moment(s) are there and then they are gone. You really need to hang on and exist within them for a long as possible, for they are so few and far between.

Let's See A Manifestation

15/December/2014 13:46

I happened upon three very rare Satya Sai Baba vinyl LPs today. I will have to give them a listen later on tonight. Finding them set me to thinking…

Sai Baba was one of those Indian Gurus who performed magic tricks. He used to do things like make ash appear from a large vessel. I personally saw Sai Baba do this in India. Even though I was very young at the time, my thought was this is just a simple parlor trick. I thought this while others around me were in awh.

Sai Baba claimed his tricks to be a product of the divine. And, his disciples believed this to be true. As time went on, more-and-more people set about debunking teachers who performed actions like this. I even remember there was this one guy who used to go on *The Tonight Show* with Johnny Carson who would perform the same techniques as these so-called holy teachers and/or healers.

As time went out, some of Sai Baba's disciples claimed that he used these tricks to draw new disciple in so that he could guide them towards enlightenment. But, a lie based upon a lie is never the truth.

Does David Copperfield claim to be a vehicle for god or enlightenment? No, he's just a great magician.

I believe that those of us upon the spiritual path, (whatever that path may be), must forever seek the truth and the truth from those who claim to teach the truth. Let's see a manifestation! And, I do not mean some foolish parlor trick. I mean, if you claim to be a vehicle towards the truth, god, and/or enlightenment, let's see you prove it. Let's see you represent god or enlightenment. Not by words but by actions. Let's see it in your life. Not by the accumulated wealth you may have acquired by falsely luring in disciples but by the action of good you have given to all things from the simplest person to the greatest whole.

Let's see a manifestation!

Gods and Superheroes

15/December/2014 08:27

I watched the film *I, Frankenstein* the other night. It was surprisingly good. It was one of the films that the trailer did not do it justice, so when it was in the theaters I let it pass by. Watching it: the CGI, the story development and evolution, and the overall presentation were all great.

The overall storyline of the film was about good verses evil. The gargoyles, which were under the guidance of Archangel Michael, were battling the demons that were under the direction of Satan. When the gargoyles died they evaporated into a white light and went towards the heavens. When the demons died they transformed to red light and went down to hell. Okay...

This film reinforced the whole concept of there are those who are greater than us common folk living on this planet. And, that is good. That is what a sci-fi film or a good sci-fi novel is supposed to do. The thing is, people use the elements presented in these films and/or writings and try to make them part of common spirituality. I mean when you think about who people worship; whether it is Jesus or whomever, they are always beings that performed these great, superhuman feats. They are superheroes.

Then, there are people who claim to be the proponents of these super humans. For me, who came up in the Eastern spiritual tradition, the gurus are forever attributed with performing great spiritual feats. In the Western spiritual traditions, many of the proponents claim to have a direct link to god. ...God or the angels speak to them and through them. The gods do this because that person is just so holy, pure, or spiritual...

If we look to case studies, in the Eastern tradition, obviously, Sri Ramakrishna suffered from schizophrenia. But, as his mind was turned towards the positivity of spirituality and not the negative realms that schizophrenia can also invoke; and because he lived in India where the crazier you are the holier you are, he was embraced as a great spiritual teacher and not simply considered insane. In the Western tradition, a person like Edgar Cayce comes to mind. He claimed the ability to enter a trance state and produce answers from the great beyond. In his time, many a seeker went to him.

There is always this big problem with people who claim these or any spiritual abilities, however. That problem is, are these people simply lying to others or are they lying to themselves? Do they truly believe that they posses superhuman abilities or are they simply trying to make others believe that they are something more than the common person while making some money in the process? ...As their services are never free. In either case, it almost doesn't matter because the end result is the same – feeble-minded people are given a reason to believe in a person claiming supernatural powers that they do not possess. ...As no one does.

People who are living in this period of time have all been exposed to the superhuman powers held by those characters in comic books, on TV, and in the movies. For those of us whose minds are drawn to spirituality, we are also told about humans who held and hold superhero powers. From this, though we obviously can't be, *"Faster than a speeding bullet. Able to leap over tall buildings with a single bound,"* like Superman, but what we can do is claim mystical powers that no one can disprove. Thus, have been born all of the mystic, the psychics, the mediums, the soothsayers, the gurus... Again, maybe these people believe their own lie, maybe they don't? But, at the end of the day, all they are doing is leading people down a road that has no end as how can anyone, who is either lying to themselves or lying to others, provide any true guidance?

We all want answers. We all want to be something MORE. We all want people to respect us. We all want to live a good life, having what we want. But, by filling our minds with nonsense that has no absolute truth or purpose, feed to us by people who's existence is more based in ego that spiritual truth, these things will never be found.

Make movies... Write novels... Create graphic novels and comic books, but don't lie to yourself or others about superhuman powers and knowledge that you do not possess. And, never believe in those who claim these abilities.

It is like the Buddha when he was asked, *"Are you a god?"* He answered, *"No, just a man." "Are you a teacher?" "No, just a man."*

The Way We Weren't

12/December/2014 08:24

I had this interesting flash, as I was getting up this morning. The song, *"The Way We Were,"* sung by Barbara Streisand, came to mind. Why, I don't know? Weird... But, the title of the song did set me to thinking...

Before I get to the whole point and realization of all of this, the thought of the song and the aftermath caused me to ponder the film. I know everyone is speaking about the upcoming film, *Fifty Shades of Grey* – which is soon to be released. But, I think the casting for that is all wrong. Dakota Johnson is no where near homely, as depicted in the book, and Jamie Dorman is not all that. They should have cast it like, *The Way We Were,* with a young Robert Redford and Barbara Streisand. That's the visual dichotomy expressed in the novel. Anyway, on to the point...

I have never been one of those people to look back at people, relationships, (failed or otherwise), and life events, and question what would have happened if only... I never felt like someone or something got away. I have always simply viewed life as life and relationships as what they were, when they were, and have moved on. This being said, in each of our lives, mine included, if I would have gone this way with that person instead of going the other, certainly my life would have turned out differently. But, different how?

I mean there were more than a few girls who came knocking on my door but I was locked up in the arms of someone else and couldn't answer. There were a few that were totally into me and I treated them like shit due to my dissatisfaction with the relationship. Not their fault, but mine. There were a couple that I was just too young and arrogant to appreciate. Others that I felt I had nothing to offer so I stepped away. There were one or two that some self-righteous, so-called friend trashed the relationship by telling them his appraisal of my truth and killed what should/could have been. And certainly, there has been a psycho bitch or two – the kind of woman that men just love because they pour a bucket of adrenaline over your head and you become enthralled in passion and all its consequences – at least for a time. Luckily, I was (eventually) smart enough to leave those women behind…

But, it is not just love affairs that define a life. It is the people(s) that you interact with and what they have the potential to do for and/or to your life. I mean, I too have been fucked over by people in business relationships. Certainly, in the martial arts there have been a few people that really messed with my life. This, after I helped them for years… The film industry, forget about it… The stories I could tell you. The future that could have been in my life had it not gotten trashed by the hands of other people more than a few times.

As I speak about my *Zen Filmmaking* buddy, Donald G. Jackson, here in this blog periodically, I can tell a story about one such incident. Don had briefly worked under the auspice of Roger Corman when he first moved to L.A. We heard that Corman was thinking about moving from film to digital for his productions. Who better to help him make this transition than Don and myself? Don set up a meet between the three of us. On the morning of that scheduled meeting, Don calls up my voice mail and tells me that he was going to the meeting alone. He stated, *"This is Donald G. Jackson and Company and you are just the, and company."* What an asshole. Fuck you! If it weren't for me, you wouldn't have finished a film in years!

For those of you who did not know him, Don was a very self-involved, selfish, childish individual. He could be a real asshole. More than a few people questioned why I was his friend. Me too…

But, I knew what was going on. Due to my age, (compared to his), my vast knowledge of technology, and my natural enthusiasm, he knew Corman would hire me and not him. I didn't speak to Don for over a year after that, though he called and called my voice mail. Finally, when he was getting near the end of his days he contacted me as he knew I was the only person who would keep his legacy alive. Which I have done. But, this is an ideal example of someone killing the what could have been in another person's life and doing it for no good reason.

In some cases, I, like everyone else, do get pissed off about what people have done to me and how it has affected my life. Like many of us, (especially in this internet age inhabited by trolls), people have said untrue things about me. Some have even written them in books and magazines. Of course, it pisses me off. And yes, it does affect the evolution and the what could have been in my life. But, you can't let yourself be defined by a retaliatory mindset – allowing people who do things like that to control your emotions. As is the case with all of us, what you do leads to what happens to you... They will get theirs.

But, back to the central premise...

The point is, and the thing we must all keep in mind: what is, is – what is not, is not. We will never know what would have been, if only... In some cases, people try to rechart their past. I know people from my past have contacted me years later to see if we can reenact a moment. You can't! Yes, it can be a different moment, if you choose it to be. But, it cannot be that ideal dream-space of what, *"Should have been,"* that is locked in your realm of fantasies.

So, ultimately we are simply in a state of living our life to the best of our ability – doing what we can with what we have available to us at this point in our Here and our Now. Yeah, our lives would have been different if... But, that is just wild speculation. It may have turned out great, if... Or, it may have turned out really shitty.

So, all we can ALL do is just live to the best of our ability. Make our choices of people, relationships, and the where, how, and who we interact with and what we do, as best as we can. Leave the past as the past and live now, with what and whom you have.

This is life. Live your moment as this moment is presented by what you have set forth in your past.

Don't look back. Look forward.

Shoreline Meditation

11/December/2014 12:04

    I was at the shoreline today – like I try to do everyday. I was standing there on this cloudy So. Cal. day anticipating the rain which is supposed to arrive fairly soon. I was staring out to the sea. There were a couple of people surfing, some people doing their powerwalks, some walking their dogs, and a bike rider or two. What caught my eye, however, was this very interesting sight. There was an elderly couple walking along and just in front of them was this California beach bird, (the Wandering Tattler), walking directly in front of them. The bird was progressing in a straight line down the walkway like he was the leader of the pack. It was perfect poetry, ideal meditation. The bird walked, the couple followed. This went on for quite a while. It was beautiful. It was perfect!

    These are the moments when life provides each of us with a gateway into the perfect interaction, the perfect synchronicity of communion with nature and the universe. It is in these moments where *satori* is born. Watch for them.

Driving On The Grey Side

10/December/2014 13:32

I think we all have our pet-peeves about things that take place when we drive. Something that really pisses us off. I know I do.

One of mine is when people who are way too old to be driving but are still behind the wheel. I mean you always hear about them thinking the gas pedal was the break and plowing into walls and through people – sometimes even killing them. Not good!!!

I had one of those old people in front of me today. They were slumped way down in their seat, trying to see over the steering wheel. And, they were driving so slow, right in the middle of two lanes, that they had build up a large convey of cars behind them. As they took up two lanes, there was no way to pass. I wanted to scream. I am sure other people behind me felt the same way. And, this whole process, with no way to pass, went on for a seemingly very long period of time.

A bit later in the day, I was walking to my car in a parking lot. This old guy in an SUV just backs out of his parking space without looking or even thinking about looking. Me, I had to jump back so he didn't hit me. He almost hit another lady, however. I yelled, *"Hey!"* But, he was too old... He didn't even care. He drove off...

Recently, I rewatched the film, *Wild in the Streets.* I first saw it when it was theatrically released in 1968. It is a great movie and one of most ideal depictions of 1960s counter culture in America -- along with *Alice's Restaurant* and *Easy Rider.* I recommend everyone see it. ...If you can find it.

The film is all about the younger people taking control of the United States. Those people who are over thirty are eventually sent to interment camps and tripped out on Acid. The thing is, one of the main points of the film is, what is the line between old and young.

But, dealing with what I did today, I decided that I would come up with my own arbitrary definition. Once your hair is totally grey, that means that you are too old and you should stop driving a car. :-)

Too Big For Their Own Britches

10/December/2014 13:13

First of all, I must state, I am a long time fan of one of the local NPR radio stations here in L.A., KCRW. As they are a public broadcast station, periodically they stop the music and beg for money for a week and a half. They do this two or three times a year.

Now certainly, I understand the need to do this. As they do not have sponsors the way most radio stations do, they need to pay their bills. To do this, they ask their listeners to give them money. For many years I used to do just that. But, then things changed...

In times gone past I was very happy to give money so the DJs and the production team could keep playing their eclectic brand of music and pay their rents. But then, they started to travel. They would fly to music events like *South By Southwest* and various other ones around the country and around the world. What that meant is that it was people like I who were paying for them to fly to these locations. And, people like I were paying for their hotels stays, in five star hotels, and for their meals.

Now, I was happy to hook them up so they could keep the music and the news playing, but I had to draw the line about paying for them to travel to places. I mean, I would love it if someone would pay for me to travel around the country and around the world. But, no one does. I'm sure you get my meaning...

This is the thing about life and giving to charities, under whatever name they title themselves... Who and what are you giving to and what are they doing with the money?

If it was just to play music and broadcast the news, I was all about it. But, not to send them on vacation.

It was like yesterday, I was walking through a parking lot to get to my car. As I have stated in the past, here in L.A., and I imagine in other cities as well, parking lots are a location where a lot of people come up to you and ask for money – for one reason or another. As I walked yesterday this African-American couple drove up to me in a very nice SUV. They rolled down their window and ask if I would give them money for gas. *"Gas!"* I wanted to say. *"If you need money for gas why are you driving around in your car? You should park it!"* But, I just smiled and told them I had no cash. Which was true. I rarely carry cash.

But... This is life... You have to be carful who you give your money to. :-)

Justice, the California Judicial System, and Let's Have Breakfast

10/December/2014 12:55

I was having breakfast at one of my long time haunts in Manhattan Beach this morning. Sitting behind was a group of three. Two of them were lawyers and one was a campaign representative. The one lawyer had hired the other lawyer because they were running for judgeship and they had not disclosed all of the money they had received from donors to run for the post or from who the money had come. I knew all of this because they were speaking very loudly.

As they spoke and discussed the interworkings of the law in California and how the one individual had violated the California Bar and what they could do about it, I could not believe they were having this conversation (loudly) in a restaurant. I mean there is absolutely no legal expectation of privacy in a location such as this. And, why would they be having this discussion in the wide open anyway?

I mean, I have had more than a few production meetings over coffee, drinks, and at breakfast, lunch, or dinner. But, those were production meetings! They were not about how someone could skirt the law and be elected a judge.

I certainly understand why so many people block out the world by having music plugged into their ears all the time. But me, I like life. I like to embrace my environment. Maybe that is the martial artist in me. I don't know? Plus, my tinnitus is way too bad from standing in front of far too many blasting Marshal amplifiers for way too many years to take the chance of making it worse.

But, what this did was to provide a unique insight, an insight that I certainly believed existed but an insight that I had no desire to hear about. ...An insight that I pass along to you.

This is life. This is politics. But, sometimes, somethings, I just don't get.... What were they thinking!

Zen Filmmaking: SS vs. DGJ

10/December/2014 08:22

I am so often asked this question that it used to annoy me, now it makes me smile... The question being, *"What is the difference between your Zen Filmmaking and that of Donald G. Jackson?"* I just got hit with that question again this morning when I was doing a Skype interview for Italy...

So, here we go again... Don, unless he was working with me, virtually always based his filmmaking around a screenplay. Me, I never do. Why did he do this? I do not know, as he was one of the most random, crazy, disorganized, discombobulated people I have ever met. He was a mess! *Zen Filmmaking* was perfect for him. But, he virtually always chose to base his films around a screenplay. Though in the press he rarely revealed this fact.

His mind-mess is what led to him starting so many films but never finishing most of them. It also led to his filming a project and then either losing the film footage or hiding it away somewhere. In some cases, he didn't even know what he did with it. This is why, while he was in the hospitable, shortly before his leaving this world, he had his wife give me all of the film and video footage he and we had filmed. He knew who and what I was, a finisher. The minute I received them, I started editing. This is why so many more films he produced or directed came out after his death than while he was alive. I still a have a few more pieces to put together over a decade since his passing.

The biggest difference between the films Don made, the films he and I made together, and the films that I make, was money. Don would get investors and some of our films had major dollars behind them. And, Don would freely spend that money. He would buy tons and tons of stuff. He would feed everybody. He would pay for everybody's gas and buy them gifts; especially if they were girls. He paid a lot of rent for a lot of young ladies... He would even pay some people.

My Zen Films are just the opposite. I never take money from investors. So, my films are made with no money.

Don and I did, however, follow the same path of spontaneous, spur of the moment production, either when we were working together or apart. We would film like we had no money, even if we did. This is what leads to the fact that it is hard to tell which of our films had a big budget and which did not.

Mostly, Don and I functioned very well as a team. Though we had very different personalities, and he did bring in a large dose of melodrama to every film we ever made together, (something that I trust is absent from my productions), we were friends and from our abstract mindset we did create some interesting pieces of filmmaking.

So, were we different filmmakers? Yes, we were. But, when we made Zen Films together the magic did occur.

Again... There, the question is answered. :-)

Talking To Hear Themselves Talk

09/December/2014 09:43

Every now and then I am simply dumbfounded when I am forced to listen to someone speak. Recently, I was at my local Starbucks, waiting at a nice outside table for my lady to bring the drinks, and there was this group of elderly woman talking and talking about the why and wherefores of interracial politics. They were so false, wrong, and misguided, it was simply scary. And, it drove me crazy, I wanted to scream. Thankfully, post going to check on what condition the drinks condition was in (as the barista was very-very slow) a professional martial artist who recognized me came out to introduce himself. Normally, I avoid those situations and claim not to be Scott Shaw but he was obviously a very nice guy so I acknowledge who I was. He introduced himself, he sat down, and we spoke. The ladies hearing him discuss my books, shut up and decided to listen to our conversation. Thank god. But, it is not always that easy.

A week or two ago I was at this gallery opening and this British lady was talking and talking and over-talking everyone in the place. Bragging about this piece of art she owned, what she thinks about the artist who was being exhibited, and so on. Everyone kept looking over at her and/or moving away from her. But, she didn't get the hint. I guess just some people love the sound of their own voice. But, other people don't. Shut up!

So-called spiritual people… I won't even go into that. They are so full of their own all-knowing bullshit that I just cannot stand to be around them. All they do is speak the same regurgitated words, giving the same bullshit explanations about life, that they heard or read somewhere else from somewhere else. It just drives me nuts. They are generally so full of their own self-righteous bullshit that this fact alone should cause them to take the hint and shut up. But, they don't. Ego driven, they simply destroy the world of true spirituality by their talking. They should be ashamed of themselves!

In fact, all this reminds me of a chapter I wrote for the book, *"Zen and Modern Consciousness,"* a few years ago about talking and saying nothing. Here it is. I will finish up this rant with that little piece, titled, *"Planned Parenthood."*

* * *

I was driving home from having lunch in San Pedro; listening to, *Jonesy's Jukebox,* on the radio. Steve Jones, probably most noted for being the guitar player in the *Sex Pistols,* hosts this radio show.

Normally, when he has guests, they are musicians. But, this day there were two girls who were talking about New Age philosophy.

They proceeded to discuss reincarnation. They stated the reason we keep reincarnating is that each time we are sent to a new physical body is because of the fact that we want to learn a very specific thing about life. They continued, of course, we don't realize this until we die and then, once we have left our physical body, we can analyze whether or not we actually learned the knowledge that we had hoped to acquire. They also stated that what takes place before we enter our current body is that we each, (somewhere up there, in some ethereal heaven), actually choose the parents that we are born to in order to actualize our path of specific knowledge acquisition.

I listened for a few moments and then changed station. I was just dumfounded by the borrowed knowledge that they were spewing – words that had been regurgitated by so many others before them. I mean, since the moment I entered the spiritual path, all those years ago, I have heard versions of that same nonsensical discourse spoken by those who want to appear spiritual – hoping to sound as if they know some deep-dark secret about the origin and evolution of life. What nonsense.

This is the problem with the novice on the spiritual path – they believe everything that they hear and then they want to repeat it. Most, however, never leave this novice level of spiritual consciousness and, thus, never rise to a state of true wisdom. This is why they simply continue to repeat what they heard – be it true or false.

But, let's take a minute here and think about what those two ladies were saying. They claim that we each choose our own parents before we are born. If this is the case, it means that our parents have no choice in the matter. They are simply infested with a soul that has chosen them. If this were true, that would mean that only the ethereal-bound entities have the right of choice and the living are simply the receptacles of the desires of the ethereal being that want to use them as the vehicle to learn what they desire to learn. If you were to believe this explanation it would detail that the ethereal beings are simply desire bound entities that are seeking something – good or bad and are using the bodies, in association with the physical, psychological, and the sociological makeup, of the earth bound parents to provide them a pathway to fulfilling their desired ends.

This is the problem with humanity as a whole. Instead of seeking the truth from within, humans concoct ridiculous abstract rational for the meaning of life. Then, the design elaborate philosophic rational to explain why these developed ideologies are happening. And, this previously described discourse is just one example. Each religion and philosophy, throughout time, has designed its own set of ridiculous tenets that it then claims to be the truth and orchestrates intricate stories so that they can claim it has factual possibilities.

Seriously, if one existed in the ethereal, heavenly realm, why would they need to return to earth and this physical existence to learn anything? Aren't the ethereal, heavenly realms the source point for all knowledge? I mean, come on, if you are in the ethereal realm and have the ability to do things like choose your parents, which means you have dominion over humans, why would you need to learn anything from the human race?

But, this is the human condition; we want to explain the abstract realms of, *"Why."* But, *"Why,"* will never be explained.

From the dawn of human consciousness to the end of it, there were and will be those who claim to know. But, if what they knew was the absolute truth, there would be no question and no other, *"Knower,"* would ever be claiming a different set of religious possibilities or stating that what another person believes is false.

Knowledge is a personal perspective. What you know is what you know. But, be careful; don't confuse what you believe with what you know, because they are two completely different things.

Ultimately, we all just are. If you can accept that it is not important to know all of the answers of the universe, then you are free. If you are free then you don't have to recite someone else's brand of borrowed knowledge. From this, the nonsense of humanity is laid to rest and all of humanity becomes free.

Zen is Free.

Round and Round

09/December/2014 08:45

A relationship, be it interpersonal or romantic, is based upon the actions and the interactions of two people. A relationship is forever based on what took place yesterday. What takes place today may be good, bad, or ugly, but what takes place today is based upon what previously took place yesterday.

People move towards being friends or lovers with a person for very specific reasons. All of those reasons are based upon desire. The desire for sex, the desire for interpersonal contact, the hope of love, the belief that being in a relationship with a specific person will lead to a specific end-goal...

As all people base their lives upon desire, (whether they understand this fact or not), they do what they do to achieve the end-goal they desire. It is for this reason that many people lie to people to make themselves look bigger, better, or more and they listen to people because they believe that by listening to that person, that person may like them.

What was said or done yesterday comes to define today. If what was said or done yesterday was caring and giving, then today may be a great day for the furtherment of good things within the relationship. If what was said or done yesterday was based upon ego, deception, or a lie, the today of a relationship may be confrontational and in jeopardy.

It if for this reason that people who are angry at their friend or partner are always angry about the same thing. Thus, the same words are spoken and the same anger is expressed. And, that anger is generally justified. The person who is the part of the relationship who is the focus of the anger generally did something wrong. They lied, they deceived, they played mind games, they pretended to be something they were not or possess some attribute or possession that they did not have. Thus, the anger, the words spoken, and the negativity within the relationship go round and round. You either speak the same words or hear the same words over and over and over again.

There is no absolute cure for a relationship in crisis. What you did, you did and you should own it, apologize for it, and try to fix it, but your ego will probably not let you do that. So, you and the relationship are stuck.

From this, people move between relationships; generally criticizing the person they left behind. But, all things in this life are your fault. Either you were the instigator of the deception or you were the believer of. So, who is to blame? Yes, you should probably stop yelling at the person who wronged the relationship but sometimes you need to let it out. The thing to remember is, the other person probably won't care. By letting them know they were the, *"Doer,"* provides them with power and ego. This is why people generally move forward though life doing and redoing the same thing over and over again. Few people are consciousness enough to see their folly and fix anything that they have broken – as their ego will not let them.

So, this is life. Welcome to the world of relationships. Do with it/with them what you will. But remember, to be the MORE not the LESS of any relationship you are in.

What Time Is It?

05/December/2014 08:32

A couple of years ago I needed a new clock. When I brought it home and plugged it in I was surprised to find out that it would set itself. For example, if the power goes out or if you unplug it and then plug it back in, or anything like that, give it a few minutes and the time will be set.

The thing is, when I look at that clock, the time is a few minutes different from the time that is presented on my computer, which also sets itself automatically. Then, if I look at my cell phone the time is also slightly different. My TV, the same thing. Close, but not exact.

Time… All set automatically. Yet, all the sources present a different time.

In truth and actuality, what time is it?

Fellini is Everywhere

04/December/2014 07:55

I always find it interesting that whenever people want to describe a strange or unique situation they say something to the effect of, *"It's like a Fellini movie."* Meaning, everyone seems to think that films created by Federico Fellini are weird and strange. Are they? Not so much. I don't think so. Yes, they have a certain visual style and curious elements placed within them. But, believe me, there are a lot weirder filmmakers out there, including myself. Anyway, since it is such an accepted term, I will use it as the title for this piece...

A few days ago I was driving down Hawthorne Boulevard. There was a lot of street re-construction going on and traffic was jammed. I noticed this one Goodwill store, so I thought I would take a break from the traffic and go inside.

The moment I walked in the first thing I notice was this very large Latino guy. Large in terms of his girth not his height. He was maybe five-four and two hundred and fifty pound. He was wearing what looked to be dirty stained clothing and he was rocking a three-day-old greying beard.

He was standing there in the electronics section of the store. He had apparently taken one of those all-in-one CD, radio, phonograph players off of the shelf and had sat in precariously upon a barstool. He had a stack of records haphazardly placed on a footstool in front of it. My first thought was he was probably checking out the record player to see if it works. No... What he was doing was taking each record, one-by-one, putting them on the phonograph and playing them for a few seconds. The thing was, the record player was sitting at an angle on the stool, so the records were skipping and not playing well. Yet, he continued.

As I walked by, he gave me a stare like I was weird. Okay... But, the management was letting this go on. So???

As I explored the store a little further I heard what sounded to be a young child speaking in a rhythmic singing style of a weird gibberish – very high pitched and impossible to make out the words. Initially, I just thought it was a child playing around, as children tend to do.

As I got closer to the sound I noticed an aging Caucasian woman dressed in a skirt and blouse. She looked very normal. I kept hearing the sound. As I got closer still to the source, I realized that it was the woman making the sound. Though she appeared very normal she was lost in some strange reality speaking and singing to herself in a language only she could understand.

It was all just very-very strange.

So, done with my looking, purchasing nothing, I headed back towards my car and the traffic jam. I gave the lady a final glance. I walked past the guy who was still playing his records who again gave me a look like I was the one who is weird.

Maybe he's right. Maybe it is I who is weird like a Fellini movie. :-)

Aftermath and the What of What You Do
04/December/2014 07:15

People rarely take the time to think about how what they are doing will effect their future and the future of others. They simply do what they do based upon whatever emotion or desire is present in any given moment. And, here arises one of the biggest hoaxes of the modern spiritual path; living in the now. It is constantly touted that living in the now is the space/place to be. It is detailed as some illusive state of mind. No. Everybody does it all the time. In fact, it is the very few who make their actions conscious and focused as opposed to desired-based or now-reactionary.

People are driven by the emotions that they feel in any given moment. That is what causes them to take action and do what they do. Damn the consequences. I am doing what I am doing.

This is place where all the aftermaths arise. You did what you did. You did what you did without caring or thinking about the impact on your life or the life of others but then there is a price to pay.

Some people continually try to do good things. And, that is a good thing. They don't speak negative words about people. They try to help instead of hinder. But, as the old saying goes, no good deed goes unpunished. This is simply the state of being in life; helping one person may hurt another. ...Doing something that you see as good and right, someone else may view as a negative action.

Certainly, doing knowingly bad things, making negative statements about people and life situations, and not caring who you hurt is never a righteous act. But, at this level of life interaction, the people who behave in this manner should expect to experience the repercussions. But, do they? Most of the time, no. They believe they will skate through, they will get away with it, and no one will be the wiser. But, people were hurt. So, how can there be no aftermath?

What you do and how you do it will come to be the defining factors of your life. How you will come to be defined is actualized by the consciousness of the actions you take. Think about this, when you have done something unthinking and in the spur of the moment that created a wave of hurtful negativity farther down the road of your life, would you have done it if you had thought it through instead of simply acting out on whatever desire or emotion you possessed in that moment?

People make excuses for their actions. People find justifications for their actions. People try to blame others for their actions. But, they only do that when they experience the aftermath of their actions.

If you do something/anything there will be repercussions. What do you want the repercussions that will come to define your life and your lifetime to be? What they will be is defined by how much you thought about what you did before you did it. ...By how much you thought about others before you thought about yourself.

Step out of the Now and enter the world of consciously thinking and discrimination. If you live your life at this level, the aftermath will be so much more enjoyable.

Energy and the Adverse of the Abstract
03/December/2014 13:03

I really don't like to talk about energy. It is one of those subjects that all the wanta-be new age gurus conjure up, stating this person has that energy or that thing has this energy. Bullshit! People have a personality and a thing is just a thing. It is you who decides whether you like them/it or you don't.

This being stated, we are surrounded by a world of people. Some of these people bring us joy but many bring us just the opposite. In fact, let's think about this for a moment. ... Make it personal. Do you set about on a course to make people's lives happier, more joyous, and better? Or, do you do the opposite? Are you so locked into yourself, your own desires, your own emotions, and your own sense of all-knowing righteous that you believe you have the right to judge, injure, or bring other people grief? The answer is yours to provide. The question is, why?

But, let's get to the point... People bring us joy or sorrow. Many times that joy or that sorrow is attributed to an object. It may be something that someone gave us and when we look at it, we remember the moment, and feel really happy. Or, it may be just the opposite. A person hurt us while we were sitting on that object. A person broke that item we really like and though we have tried to glue it back together it has never been the same so every time we look at it we feel hurt, and so on... Then, that object presents negative memories. The energy is no longer the subject of abstraction; it is something real and concrete.

For example, on a personal note, I have this really shitty neighbor, who was so loud, thoughtless, and full of his own bullshit when he moved in next to me that I had to move the most favorite desk I ever owned from one room to the next simply so I could get anything done. The trouble was, in the move, the desk somehow tweaked and all the ball bearings fell out of the keyboard drawer. From that point forward, out of nowhere, the drawer would periodically fall on my lap when I was working at the desk. It really pissed me off and it made me continually think about what a loud rude asshole my neighbor was. I dealt with it for a year or two or something like that until yesterday I purchased a new desk. Finally, I got rid of my old desk. What a freeing experience. Though I miss the desk, as I really loved it and it was perfect.

...And, though I never found another one, even though I have looked and looked, no longer am I burdened by the continued thoughts or negativity brought about by the situation my rude neighbor created.

This is the point. Things don't have energy. What things do is to remind us of what took place; back when. If what took place was good, great. Keep that object, cherish it, remember the moment by embracing it. But, if things make you remember less than ideal times in your life, it is best to cut them loose.

Relinquishing the Power

03/December/2014 08:16

Everyone wants something else – something more out of life. Everyone wants their life to be better in some way. From this, people have turned to others who claim to hold the power of providing that desired end. People turn to everyone and everything from psychics, to *feng shui* experts, onto gurus. Each claims to hold some mystic truth that will fill the void that you perceive in your life and help you achieve what you desire. They promise to pass their knowledge onto you. Some do it in books, other do it via talks and seminars. But, there is one common factor to this equitation. That common factor is, you are relinquishing your power, you are allowing others to guide you and take control over you.

There is one fact that people commonly forget when they turn to others for guidance, that fact is, each person is their own person, they are defined by their own desires and are cursed by their own demons. The more one claims to have no demons, the more one claims to be a conduit of perfection and divinity, the bigger liar they are. Thus, you are giving yourself over; you are relinquishing your power to someone who is no better than you and, in fact, is most probably far less honest than you, they may simply be more outgoing and possess a greater ability to play the game of teacher than you, but that does not mean they are more all-knowing or any better than you.

Like I always say, *"If you love hell it becomes heaven,"* if you relinquish your desire(s), you are free. But, most of us are not like that. We still want what we want. We believe that if we have THAT our life will be better.

To end the relinquishing and to truly take control over your own life and your own being you must first and foremost realize that no one is totally fulfilled, no one has all that they want, no one does not feel the same emotions as you. Some simply lie and pretend that they do not.

Therefore, study what you want to learn. Consciously move towards what you desire. Place yourself in situations where the opportunities to move towards what you ultimately hope to become exist. But, never believe that another person can provide you with your ultimate dream. That task is left solely on your shoulders.

You Probably Wouldn't Even Like Me

02/December/2014 09:51

We have all heard the stories of people meeting via the internet. Some meetings have turned out to be great while many others have turned out to be not so nice. Some have led to love. While other have led to insane stalker situations.

We have all also heard about the people who lie about who they truly are via the internet. Some of us have experienced that. TV shows like Catfish have done a great job of depicting this crisis. We have also heard about all the trolls who live at their parent's house and say all kinds of nasty, mean-spirited things about people on the internet. What a waste... Like someone reminded me when I read a passage they wrote on a website, inhabited by trolls, that were falsely bashing me. (BTW If you're gong to talk shit, at least know the truth and speak the truth otherwise you make yourself look stupid). Anyway... The person wrote, *"Like your grandmother told you, if you don't have anything nice to say, don't say anything at all."* I believe each of us should hold fast to that motto.

Anyway... With all this as a basis, I have long wondered how anybody trusts anyone they meet via the internet.

As one of those people who has been on the internet before it was even called the internet, I have watched all of this process occur. And, it is interesting. Me, I love the internet. But, meeting via the internet. Well...

This being said, by my nature I am a very friendly person. So, I am always all-about meeting nice people. But, the thing about this is, in life, there are personalities. When you initially meet a person, on a face-to-face basis, you can quickly decide, do you want to spend any time with them or not. Via images and conversations on the internet, not so much.

Because I am who I am, I am frequently invited to meet with people, go to functions, and the like, via the internet. Also, me being who I am, I commonly turn these invitations down. Art gallery openings; sure, I may show up. Movie premieres, sometimes. Music; not so much. I am tired of having my ears blown out by bad bands. Face to faces; rarely. Why? Because you probably wouldn't even like me and I probably wouldn't even like you. Some people are very real so you can kind of have an idea about what they are and/or are not. Others, not so much...

Some people still smoke. Can you believe that? When I meet people who are that unconscious – that is the end of that. I mean, if you don't care about your own health or the health of those around you, why would I want to be your friend? But, moreover, people want things. They expect me to do things for them. Things that I just cannot do. Yet, the never tell me that when they set up a meet. Has this happened to you?

Like I joking tell people, *"If it's a pretty girl who wants to have meaningless sex with me, then I'm there... But, other than that..."* :-) ...Other than that, it is just so weird...

What I have found, over-and-over again, is that ninety-nine percent of the people who contact me never bring anything to the table when they want to meet me. No one ever contacts me to offer me anything. All they want to do is meet and then take. Why is that? Does this happen to you? Whenever I interact with anyone, I want to give them something; not take anything away.

I don't get it? Is life all about wanting and taking? Or, is life about giving?

Overall, life is a funny place, especially now in the world of cyberspace. The thing about it is, it is all smoke and mirrors. Everything is an illusion propagated by the internet. The only real is the real of real life. Where do you live your life?

Anyway, this is just my ramble for the morning...

Work With What You Have

02/December/2014 08:30

When I was operating my first martial art studio in association with a master I had helped emigrate here from South Korea, like most studios we had a lot of teenage students. I remember this one young man who was very tall, maybe six foot seven, and still in high school.

During this period we also had a lot of young taekwondo practitioners, newly arrived from South Korea, who would come to train. There was this one young man who could do those beautiful, perfect, aerial kicks. He had been training since he was a young child and he was one of those who had the gift.

It was the end of class and as we traditionally did I sat the students down and pull them up in pairs for a little light contact sparring. As the two previously described students were about the same age, I called them up. I had them bow and set them to sparring. The Korean student delivered a few well-placed kicks to his very tall opponent. I guess the tall student was tired of the other student penetrating his defenses. He moved in and grabbed the guy. He then literally picked him up and body slammed him to the floor. I rushed in, *"No, no, no!"*

Now, this was at a time long before the arrival of Brazilian jujitsu, which led to the Ultimate Fighting Championships, which led to MMA, which has taken over the globe. We were a traditional Korean martial art studio.

The young man up off the floor, I paired them off again. I set them to fighting. Same scenario, the Korean guy delivered some well-placed kicks and bam the guy using his size and his weight grabs him, lifts him up, and slams him to the floor. *"You can't do that,"* I tell him. *"Why? That's what I do in wrestling at school,"* he replies.

Though I had to stop the fight, the truth be told, I appreciated what the young man did. What he did was to use what he had to defeat a superior opponent. This is what the true martial arts is all about.

You see, this is the thing... There is tradition and then there is what works. At our school we wanted our students to train their bodies in the kicks and self-defense of the traditional Korean martial arts. Though I certainly understood, even way back then, that mixing and combining techniques of various martial art systems made a person a more complete martial artists, (I mean that is what I was doing with hapkido and taekwondo), but as it was a traditional school, we had to teach traditional techniques via the traditional methodology.

Though traditional schools of the martial arts still abound, the thought process has greatly shifted over the past thirty years. Now, integration and using what works is the understood name of the game. And, this is as it should be.

This is the same in life. We each have our gifts and we each have our deficits. Some of us our tall, some of us can do beautiful kicks, some of us have no definable attributes but, none-the-less, we are unique onto ourselves. What we must do as we chart our way through life is to critically define what we can and cannot do and then work with what we have to become the best that we can be; defeating any obstacles by constantly adapting.

Tension in the Air

01/December/2014 13:17

I was in the hood today, scouting a new location for my next Zen Film and/or Music Video and it was a strange experience, there was a certain palatable tension in the air. Or, maybe better put, there was a tension brought about by certain people.

I imagine this goes back to all the havoc that is taking place, based on what went on in Ferguson. But, none-the-less, it was/is interesting to witness.

It first came to my attention when this kind of rough looking black guy pulls up to a four way stop on a side street a little bit after me but proceeds to go though the stop sign. He looks at me like I am at fault. He gives me this hard look, like, *"Look out."*

This kind of person always amuses me. ...The one's who think that they can intimate people by looking mean, those who walk with a swagger, and those try to play hard. I mean, those guy have already lost the fight. If they could fight, they wouldn't behave like that. But anyway...

What occurred next was even funnier, as he drove through the intersection, under his breath of the rolled down window of his junky Japanese sedan, he voiced, *"White mutha fucka."* Wow, I have not been called a racial epithet in L.A. since I can't remember when.

I think that what is going on right now is that people, who base their lives upon anger and negativity, are using the Ferguson situation to motivate themselves to act out on their anger. But, destruction never proves anything. Especially when it is destruction brought to the doorstep of innocent people.

As I said in a previous blog on this subject, some people are just looking for a reason to be mad. And, though many of us, myself included, have a certain underlying anger at life and/or modern society, we known how to utilize that emotion to a positive end. These other people do not seem to know how to do that.

A short time later I was walking though this parking lot when these two African-American guys who both rocked Afros straight out of the 1970's walked past me and said, *"Nice day isn't it?"* They said this in an obviously facetious, antagonizing manner. I looked at them and smiled. *"Oh, you're a funny one, aren't you,"* they stated.

Just amusingly weird...

One of things I took note of, as I was driving around the hood was, that when I went to school in Southcentral is was virtually all African-American. A bit later, a lot of Latin peoples moved into the area, as well; making it more racially diverse. But, now, there is also a noticeable about of Caucasian people walking and driving around. This is a very interesting sociological process taking place, I believe – how the area continues to make racial changes. If I had the time or if I was still full-time at a university, I may do a study, a history-based study of the population demographics of the region. But, as I am not...

You know, it is like when my father grew up in Southcentral and went to *Manual Arts High School* in the mid 1930s, I remember him telling me how it was a racially mixed area. Then, when I lived there, it was predominately Black and the *Watts Riots* and all that jumped off. And now, in the process of re-mixing...

All this being said, there still remains an obvious amount of racial tension that is simply waiting for a moment for it to express itself and erupt. Interesting... I thought/hoped we were past that. I guess not.

Speaking of my father, when I was driving away from the hood, I passed by the cemetery where he was buried in 1968. I hadn't been to his grave for years, so I thought I would stop by. I found his gave and the graves of the rest of my family. Then, I noticed the grave next to his. The person had died in 1928. It made me think that whoever even knew or cared about that person is long gone. And, after I die, there will be no one left who remembers or cares about my family.

Cemeteries... It just seems like such a momentary thing that should not last for centuries. What end, do they serve?

Repetition

01/December/2014 07:36

When you live in the world of the martial arts like I do, one of the primary teaching strategies is repetition. And, this is true with all art forms that teach patterns and process; whether that be the martial arts, ballet, or classical music. It is believed that by doing a pattern over and over again, the process becomes so integrated into an individual's mind then they can perform it without thinking. And, this is true.

There is a problem with this method, however. That problem is, some people become lost in the repetition and lose focus on the goal. The ultimate goal of these art forms is mastery over the moment – pure understanding of the movement, not simply the doing of the moment.

This is where the understanding of repetition lends its basis to life. Doing is doing. But, doing should be done with pure consciousness for this is where satori is born. Doing should not, however, be done in a mindless manner simply because one has learned how to do something and, thus, does it over and over and over again. For here, the process of repetition is where mental illness is born.

Look at a person who suffers from mental illness with a basis in obsessive-compulsive behavior; what do they do? They believe, in their distorted reality, that they must perform the same action over and over again. But, what does this mindset lead to? Does it lead to an obtained goal or physical and mental perfection? No, it only leads to quenching of the addiction of the moment that is defined by their distorted mind.

If a person allows their life to fall into a mindless repetition, it is far different from a focused, meditative repetition. If your repetition controls you, compared to you controlling it and your using it as a means to obtain an ultimate goal, then it is mental illness not meditation.

The subtitles of life and how they impact a person's actions and interactions with life is what set the conscious person apart from those who are simply controlled by the random, oftentimes, misguided thoughts of their human mind. Who are you?

Emotional Projection

30/November/2014 08:38

People who are happy look for a reason to smile.

People who are hateful and angry look for a reason to be mad.

People who allow themselves to be defined by any hurt they may have experienced seek a reason to make others feel the way that they do; hurt.

Though we each feel emotions based upon our life experiences, how do you project those emotions to the world? Do they define you or do you define them?

Emotions are projected by what you say and what you do. These projections define your personal interaction with the world and tells all people who you are.

Who are you?

VHS

28/November/2014 08:07

In recent years there has been a large underground resurgence for cassette tapes of music. In fact, there are a few record companies that now release music only on cassette tape. That's cool.

To many, that is simply attempting to resurrect an era gone past as everything is all-about the digital now. But, there is a sound that is possessed by analogue that simply does not exist digitally. But, in all honesty, very few can hear that different or even care. Times move on...

Recently, I've been reinvestigating my VHS collection. Though the truth be told, years ago I gave away most of it to thrift shops. But, some still remain. And, every now and then I find a new one that I want to watch or rewatch.

Recently on my VHS deck has been *Phantom of the Paradise, Zachariah, The Swimmer, Attack of the Mushroom People, Slaughter in San Francisco, Sugar Town, The Double Life of Veronique, Juliet of the Spirits,* and *Psychomania.* All great, must watch films. Some you can find out there on DVD or for digital download, some you cannot. But, watching them digitally really misses the point as they were each created long before digital existed.

There is simply something great about watching a movie that is not perfect like it often is in HD. It is great to see the graininess of it, observe the video echoes, and the problems with sound and/or tracking. It makes the sensory experiences so much more whole.

When the world of indie film creation switched over from VHS to DVD many people were mad at me that my newer films were no longer available on VHS. A few are still out there and you can pick them up but many are not. And, I can make you a one-off if you really want one. But, the fact was, it simply became so much cheaper and far less time consuming to distribute the films digitally. With that, something was lost. I do understand. Me too, I miss VHS.

Though I doubt there will ever be the VHS resurgence as there is for cassettes, for those of you of the younger generation who have never watched a movie on VHS, I suggest you give it a try, it will open up a whole new level of artistic understanding. And, for those of you who do remember the era, I suggest you take a look back, give it another try. Remember the remembering...

Sometimes the lack of perfection is the perfection.

Missing the Mood of the Moment

27/November/2014 08:42

In this period of civil unrest I believe that a lot of people are missing the mood of the moment. Instead of seeing it as a time to orchestrate change for the better they are simply using it as a time to puff up, show how big and bad they are, and orchestrated disruption to innocent people and unleash violence.

If we look to history, and the great purveyors of peaceful civil unrest, first and foremost, we think of Mahatma Gandhi. But, let's look at his legacy. Yes, the British Empire was caused to leave India. But, during that process the violence that occurred to protestors and throughout the Indian civilization was immense. Then, the moment the Crown left so much bloodshed and violence erupted that it was unparalleled at any other point in India's history. What occurred was the creation of two separate countries: India and Pakistan, that are still at odds with one another. And, like I have said many times, even today, India is one of the most violent places on earth.

So, who won and who lost? And, how many innocent people had their lives ruined by the actions of the greater powers and the people simply looking to bring violence and cause hurtful disruption?

When the stepfather of the young man at the center of the controversy in Ferguson was screaming, *"Burn this bitch down,"* over and over again a few nights ago, I think we can understand his motivation but we can also see the source point for the violence that occurred. Perhaps we can even see the influence that guided the young man to commit the strong-arm robbery that set it all in motion.

Do the people that are unleashing the havoc truly care about anything or do they simply want a reason to riot?

Most of us are mad a society at some level or another. We each have bones to pick. But, change does not come about through meaningless violence, nor does it happen by doing stupid things like going onto a freeway and blocking the traffic of people who are simply trying to get to work to survive and pay their bills. The people that are doing that are not seeking change they are simply asking to be put into the spotlight. Thus, their actions are all about ego, not change.

How does getting arrested, which will affect the rest of your life, change anything? How does damaging people's cars or destroying and looting small businesses change anything? It only hurts people. It hurts the average person. Not the powers that be.

I think back a number of years ago when celebrity protestors used to protest against nuclear power plants. Sure, they are dangerous. But, how many of those celebrities were getting at least some of their electrical power from those plants? As this was long before solar energy. It was just a, *"Here, look at me,"* ploy.

The celebrities got arrested, as did other people. But, the nuclear power plants remained. In fact, it wasn't until 2012 when the *Nuclear Regulatory Commission* closed down San Onofre because it was prematurely falling apart.

If you want change, do it without ego. If you want change, do it in a way that does not hurt the average person. If you want change, do it in a way that helps everybody, then everyone will be onboard with you.

Stop the damage. Stop the hurting. Orchestrate change through positive action.

Art For Art Sake Equals No Money

26/November/2014 08:52

In each of our lives we do what we do on a daily basis but then certain specific periods become defined by certain specific things that we are doing.

Recently, I've been seeing a lot of art. In fact, this has been pretty happenstance. For though I forever seek out great art and great artists, recently it has just been coming my direction. Why? Your guess is as good as mine.

Anyway, I was having a discussion with this one lady at a gallery I was at recently and through it I realized how a lot of the art, though it may be very-very good limits its audience due to its subject matter. For example if you look at the paintings of Bob Dylan, (yes, the Bob Dylan), his primitive style of visual-scapes is very pleasing to the eye, if you are into that type of abstract art. I am. There is nothing offensive about it. It can be hung anywhere. But then, there are those artists, (myself included), who frequently go to the nude female form. But, are people going to hang that on their wall and invite their grandmother over or hang it if they have kids? Probably not.

And, this is the thing; an artist does what an artist does due to their interpretation of the world and how they want to present that interpretation to viewers. But, if that interpretation is abstract, you lose many viewers. If it presents erotica, you lose a lot more, and so on.

Each artist must ask themselves, is it art for art sake or would you prefer to make some money? That must be answered on an individual basis.

Obviously, we all know the answer I came up with. Everything I do creatively is weird and few have the eye for it. I guess that's why I have no money. :-)

Angry Affluent White Kids

25/November/2014 08:00

Well, after the verdict jumped off in Ferguson last night, as was expected, the city blew up. What I thought was interesting is that the people didn't even wait to hear the whole press conference – which was a bit long. The St. Louis County Prosecuting Attorney should have held the findings to the end. But, he gave them out early on, thus nobody listened to the reason why.

Now, I am not going to discuss my opinion about the Grand Jury decision because we all have our own. What I will say is a few things about my personal experiences as I have been in the middle of more than one riot and have had some interaction with police officers. And, for the record, I am not going to talk about when I was in Tiananmen Square in '89 because that's a whole other situation onto itself.

First of all, the kid strong-armed robbed a storeowner before everything happened. Had he not done that, none of this would have gone on. He set it in motion. But, everybody seems to forget that. Then, he punched a cop through the window of his police car multiple times when his description had been put out over the airwaves. Believe me, if someone is punching me through the window of my car and I have a gun, I am going to shoot 'em like the cop did. I believe most of us would do the same. And, the evidence shows the cop never shot him in the back as was reported by the press. Who started it all forever equals who is ultimately to blame. That is the ultimate lesson of life.

Okay... Now to experience(s). I lived in the middle of Southcentral when the 1965 Watts Riots jumped off. Why my father would leave my mother and I, the only white family in the neighborhood, home alone when he went to run his restaurant, is beyond me. But, as we lived on a main street, I saw all the National Guard troop carriers and armored cars driving past and was, of course, watching the carnage on TV. Luckily, we made it through okay. But, it was scary...

I've told this story before but when Martin Luther King Jr. was assassinated, it was me, the only white kid in the school, that they gangs were coming to kill at the end of the day. It must be my fault, right? My African-American classmates gleamed as the day went on as they each happily told me, *"They are coming to get you."* Luckily, the police heard the rumors, as well. Maybe informed by one of the teachers and they came and took me home. Thus, I was saved from the long walk home.

I was listening to a radio DJ, Larry Mantle, a couple of months ago, who has done a show, *AirTalk,* here in L.A. on KPPC forever. He's about my age. He described how when he was teenager a cop had put a gun to his head and told him, *"I could kill you right now and no one would even question why."* I never knew of another white person who that had happened to them besides me. Nice to hear I wasn't the only one. Yes, yes... In my teenage years, I was a bit of a delinquent. I also got arrested a couple of times. What I learned is that if you are nice and cool with the cops, they will be cool with you.

Back in the punk days we used to hang out at this nightclub call the Starwood. The thing that was strange about it was they had this whole longhaired thing in one room and a punk thing in the other. Bad mix. The punks hated the longhairs and there were always fights. One night, I was there with my two friends who were brothers. One of them got into it with a longhair. Just as he was about to punch him, I see the cops pull up out of the corner of my eye. I tried to tell him to stop but it was too late. Bam, he hit the guy, putting his nose on the other side of his face. The cops jump out, grab my friend. His brother tries to run up and help him. *"That's my brother,"* he screams. I hold him back. The cops seeing I'm the only one with a level head tell me to hold him back or he will be shot. I exclaim to him, as I held him back, *"You don't fuck with the cops!"*

Again, the person who started the situation, my friend, was responsible for its ultimate outcome and what did or did not happen.

1992, the L.A. riots jumped off. Me, I was scheduled to film, *Samurai Vampire Bikers from Hell.* The traffic on the 405 was a mess so I get off to take the streets up to Hollywood. I drove right through the intersection where Reginald Denny had been beaten in the head with a brick. It could have been me. I just showed up at the moment when it had calmed down before it all went crazy and a massive riot broke out. We were filming and my pager kept blowing up. It was my lady telling me the city was on fire and to get out, the riot was on.

Last night, I watched on CNN as the rioters in Ferguson looted stores. They even burned down a storage facility. All those people who had nothing to do with anything lost all their positions over hooliganism. How do these actions help anything or make anything any better? No, they do not!

Last night, in L.A., a bunch of angry affluent white kids broke onto the 110 freeway and shut it down. They're probably students at USC – a very expensive school in a crappy neighborhood. The press goes up to one angry affluent white kid, he states, *"I'm angry that it did not even go to trail."*

Here's the thing, obviously this kid does not even understand the judicial process in America. These types of events don't just go to trail. They must pass though a Grand Jury to decide if there is enough evidence to prosecute. Then, even if it did go to trail, what is the verdict come out, innocent? Another reason for a riot?

People are angry at life. Me too. There is a lot of not right on both the personal and the societal levels going on. But destruction, due to anger, especially when it is the destruction and disruption of other people's lives, is never the answer.

Obviously, this situation is not going to be over for a while. There will be a lot of talking heads talking about it for a long time to come. And, who knows the ultimate outcome. This being said, if you want to know the source of everything/anything look to the original causation factor. There lies the answer of who is to blame?

Only If You Want It and You Know What It Is
25/November/2014 07:59

This past Sunday, after my lady and myself had breakfast at this fun little bistro I discovered in the LBC. Afterwards, we headed over (as we tend to do) to an Antique Faire as they bill it. Basically it is just a flea market with a better name.

She was looking at the jewelry created by this one lady she is a fan of and me, I was looking at this guy's wears a few spaces over. Just as I discover this one item he was selling, the proprietor tells the guy in the booth next to him that he is going to hit the head and could he watch over his space. He walked away...

Now, let me flash back maybe fifteen years ago or so. That was a time when eBay had just hit the scene. It was a great way to clean house and make some money while doing it.

Throughout the late eighties and well into the twenty-first century I was an avid road bike rider. I would do the minimum of twenty-five miles on most nights of the week. I would kick it until about eleven in the PM and then hit The Stand on one of my racing bikes and put in some distance. In fact, there was even a period when I was training Olympic hopeful in bike racing, way back in the way back when.

Anyway, eBay came along. I had collected a number of bikes that I was no longer using. So, it was the time to move them along. I listed this one Italian Bianchi, in the famous Bianchi green, on eBay. A guy bought it. He came over to pick it up, as he was local. That was great, I didn't have to pack it and ship it. When he saw it he said, *"This bike is beautiful. I have wanted one since they first came out. I guess, sometimes you just have to wait to get what you want."*

Okay, flash back to the present. What I had found, that this guy was selling, was a large stereo audio power meter. Back in the late seventies when I was recording my music on a 4-track reel-to-reel, I wanted one of those so bad. But, it was just a little out of my budget. So, I never got one.

But, here it was. Brand new, in the box, never opened. But, the guy was gone...

The problem that hit my brain was, *"What is this guy going to ask for it?"* For at swamp meets the prices are all over the place. Sometime they are very reasonable and other times they are insane – people believing they have pure, vintage, gold. What to do? I waited for a few minutes but no sign of the guy.

My lady was done with her jewelry buying. I told her the score. And she, as she always does, told me to do whatever I wanted to do.

In my brain, I couldn't decide what to do, however: wait or go. I'm a Libra, okay. ...So, making up my mind is never easy. :-)

Anyway, we walked around the general area a bit, headed back, but still no sign of the guy. But, just as we were about to leave, I saw him approaching. We went back to his booth. He made apologized to all the people wondering where he had gone. I asked him, *"How much?" "Ten dollars,"* he stated. No negotiations needed. I, of course, paid him the ten bills.

So, like the guy who bought my Bianchi before me, there it was, forty years later, something I had so desired -- way back in the way back when. I finally got it!

The funny thing is, back then, in the 70s, that unit probably would have really helped me create music. It may have even changed my life. But now, technology has all changed. Though it is, of course, very cool, I don't really know what I am going to do with it??? It served needed purpose.

So, life is funny… You have to want to something to care about getting it. Getting it, even if it is forty years too late. :-)

Enlightenment... For Free

24/November/2014 08:14

Sometimes people ask me why don't I do this blog on one of those website where you get paid to blog, via the advertisements and stuff that are on the pages on those kinds of sites. Certainly, my manager is always all over me about giving thing away for free. But, that is just who I am.

I mean, don't you hate it when you go to sites like YouTube and you have to watch a commercial in front of the video you are trying to watch and stuff like that? I just usually click it off. Forget it!

Recently, I was reading a statement that Dave Grohl made saying in essence that bands should give their recorded music away for free. If they want to make money they should go play a show. That's a great ideology.

Now, I'm a fan of Grohl, the Foo Fighters, and his film work. But, there is a certain reality that must be understood; that guy is worth a quarter of a billion dollars. Between Nirvana, the Foo Fighters, etc., he has made a lot of money. So, it is easy to make a statement like that from his vantage point.

That being said, though I need to make money just like most everyone else, I try to do all I can for those who want to read the words I write by not burdening them with advertisements and, *"Donate Here,"* buttons. ...Especially, if the words I write have anything to do with spirituality.

Anyone who charges you for enlightenment, psychological, or spiritual guidance is a fraud. In all the years I spent with Swami Satchidananda, I was never charged anything. I went to a shrink for years and she never charged me a dime. How cool is that? That's the way it should be.

But, more to the point, it is all about giving, not taking.

You know, with all of the craziness out there on the internet, I know there are a lot of people who hijack other people's work and make money off it. Now, I am totally against that. That is just wrong! They didn't create it, so why should they be able to make money from it? Whether that moneymaking is via bootlegging, reviewing, or whatever, they should be more of a whole person than to rip people off and make money from someone else's creation.

All this goes back to the early days of sampling when people would sample segments of other people's music and then lay their own vocals over it. The law is very clear now; you can't do it. Not one-second without paying. And, this goes from music, to art, to words, to film, and onto everything else.

A little thing to know is that you don't have to sue people if they are using your creations to make money. All you have to do is to report them to the FBI via their internet fraud division – where you can file the complaint online. It takes them some time, but they do shut the person down and in some cases fine them major dollars.

Due to my personality, when people have ripped me off, I've let most things slide. But, I do know several people who have done this and it does work.

But, I'm off subject here… The thing is, yes you can make money on the internet. If you choose to do that, do it via your own creations; don't rip other people off and justify your actions believing that it is okay to make money off of someone else's time, work, and creativity. But, more than that, give. If you are going to do something, if you are gong to create something that is designed to be internet-friendly, then provide it for free and go and make your money somewhere else.

Give means give. Give and it will be a better world. Give what you have to give for free.

Editors Who Need Editing

21/November/2014 13:11

  I believe that most people do not understand the underlying politics that go on in the world of publishing. Most people don't write, so they never try to have their works published. But, for those who do write, few find a publication or a publishing company that will publish their work. Fewer yet, find any success if they do have their works published. This being said, for those of you who have wondered, here's a little bit of the inside goings on…

  I was having breakfast with a friend of mine this morning. He's a writer, with some success. Currently, he is trying to break into this one specific field of journalism. He was describing how he had gone out of his way to get a very specific interview, write and submitted the piece, and though it was professionally written, about a subject the editor of the publication had requested, after it was published, he was taken to task by the editor over some really bullshit nitpicking ideology that was actually the fuck up of the editor, not my friend.

  My friend, I fear, suffers from the same disease as I – he sees everyone as a friend, when most people are far from it. So, this situation, with his editor, hit him hard.

  Anyway, as he was telling his story, it made me think back to a recent episode I had with an editor, which I relayed to him. In actuality, I wrote about it in the *Scott Shaw Zen Blog 3.5,* which you can now find in the book, *Words in the Wind,* (if you want to). But, some of you may remember it. For those of you who don't, it was a very similar situation to what my friend had gone through and it may give you some insight into what to expect if you freelance for a magazine.

  …There is this one editor I have worked with for years upon years. He called me up frantic. He really needed a cover story for the magazine and he needed it yesterday. (This is generally the case whenever he calls me). All this was occurring because the guy he had planned to interview for the issue had flaked. The editor was stuck. But me, I came to the rescue. I offered an interview with my friend, the guy who was the actual creator of the whole genre that the magazine issue was to be about. The editor and I spoke about the article, he told me what he wanted, I contacted my friend, wrote the piece, and turned it in days before it was due. The editor thanked me, said the piece was great, and that was that. The issue came out, but here's the catch, the editor broke the agreement with me, (in other words he lied). He lied about the one requirement that we agreed upon if I was to bring my friend to the magazine. That requirement was my friend was to be on the cover.

It seems pretty logical. He was the cover story... But, the fact is, he didn't even mention my friend's name on the cover. But, he did use one of his artworks as the cover piece. I believe we can all agree that is messed up.

Anyway, when the magazine came out, and my friend was not on the cover, I mentioned this to the editor. Instead of saying he was sorry or anything like that, he attacked my friend, he attacked the article, and he hid from me at a convention we were both attending. And then, he lied about it in a very bullshit email he sent me days later. Luckily, I had kept all the editor's previous emails on the subject. Moreover, if he needed a new photo of my friend or anything like that, all he had to do was ask, as I'm a photographer, okay...

The situation that my writer-friend was going though and me, thinking back to my previous situation, made me reminisce back a little further about this editor. As I explained to my friend...

A few years ago, a major publishing company published one of my books. So, I had them send a copy to the editor. Instead of saying, *"Thank you,"* or anything like that, what he did was write the publishing company an email and cc'd it to me. In it he listed the books he had published and questioning why should they have even sent him my book because he was so much more than it, them, or me. What an arrogant asshole. And, as we all understand, arrogance is most often based upon insecurity. I kept a copy of that email. I look at it occasionally when I need a laugh.

But, back to the subject... What he didn't mention in that email, however, is the fact that instead of using an editor credit, like most book creators do when they have other people write their chapters for them, this guy takes full author credit. I know, because I've written chapters for his books. When I have done this for other people, they put my name on the cover. Or, in the world of academia, they put in the table of contents, chapter by… But, this guy never even paid me a dime for my research or my work on his books.

Again, I see everyone as a friend and I always hope to help my friends. So ultimately, I guess it is my own fault. But, complying and editing does not equal authorship. Yet, this guy takes the author creator. And, he made a name for himself by doing this.

Anyway… That's just background for you.

So, what does this tell you? It all goes to the bullshit of the publishing industry and the bullshit of the people who operate in that industry.

But, as I told my friend this morning, don't let this kind of behavior keep you from writing. Because now, (today), in this digital world, there are so many ways you can write without having to be dominated by assholes who don't appreciate what you do for them and, more than that, try to lie their way out of any negative situation that they, themselves, created.

Okay… That's that, just a little lesson in life. Read into it what you will. And, that's right! I want to bite the hand that feeds me. :-)

And Then No One Remembers

21/November/2014 07:30

I often bring up the fact to people to think about a TV show you really liked five, ten, fifteen years ago. Where are the stars of that show today? In many cases, they have faded from modern consciousness and if you ask people about them they question, *"Who?"*

This is the same with many sports stars. Their careers only last for a moment.

Fame is fleeting. Notoriety is fleeting. Most people have none of it. Some people have some of it. But, few can ever hold onto to any of it.

I think back six or seven years ago to when MySpace was all the rage. Some people really became MySpace Super Stars and it really moved their life forward. And, they did it by doing nothing but putting up photos and posts.

Why they changed the format of MySpace, I will never understand, as it was perfect. But, now it is all gone.

Places like facebook and twitter are not designed to make people famous. If you are famous then people will follow you. If not; well… Good luck.

But, MySpace wasn't like that. Especially girls could really make a name for themselves. You know, with all of the internet geek guys out there, hoping for a chance – believe that they may have one… Anyway, girls got famous. Then, it and they were gone. Some people launched their own website but it wasn't the same thing.

Maybe a month or so ago I bumped into one of those once famous MySpace girls up in San Francisco. Same cute, bubbly personality; but no more internet fame. Her Esty store isn't selling like it once was and she had to go and get a job-job.

I knew other girls from back then who used to put up photos and videos of themselves shot in their bedroom. Though most of the posts weren't sexual in anyway, I think we all understand the though that a bed behind a girl puts in the minds of certain young men. I joked with all of them, *"Is that a set or is that actually your bedroom?"*

Life is funny place/space. People want notoriety. People want to be loved. People want to be desired. Some actually work towards that end and do something with their life. Most only dream. But, here is the reality of the reality; if you don't keep movin' up, if you don't keep changing with the times, if you don't find a way to keep you face and your name out there, then you will be gone. And, people will question, *"Who?"*

Sadly, there is no longer a One Stop Shop for instant fame like MySpace.

Zen Filmmaking 1973

20/November/2014 09:03

Flipping channels, the great Blaxploitation film, *Black Caesar* was just starting on one of the movie channels last night. With nothing else on worth watching, my lady and I took the time to rewatch the film. Good movie! I remember first seeing it when it was theatrically released back in '73 at one of the theaters on Hollywood Blvd. (Back then, my friend Steve and I would walk down the street and ask the person in the ticket booth if we could get in for free. Whomever would let us in, that is what we would see. We didn't need to do that. We had money. But, for whatever adolescent logic, that is what we would do). Anyway...

One of the interesting things I noticed that I had completely forgotten about was that when they were filming this movie they must have been doing it *Zen Filmmaking* style – with no filming permits. For if you watch the scenes shot on the streets in New York City near the end of the film, where Fred Williamson's character is shot, he is walking around and everyone is looking at him, looking at the camera, trying to figure out what is going on as he is supposedly bleeding – walking around all injured and stuff. It is pretty amusing. You can even see one guy walking up to him and trying to help him.

Now, I don't know the actual facts about the filming of this movie but it is a very interesting experiment in crowd interaction. And, I guess the director, Larry Cohen, was willing to have, and/or did not care about, the crowd looking into his lens. ...As we all understanding this is the absolute no-no in traditional filmmaking.

When you compare this movie to arguably the best Blaxploitation film ever, Super Fly, you can see the budgetary differences. When Ron O'Neal's character, Priest, was interactive in NYC he didn't have the staring into the camera of the massive by-passers going on. More budget obviously buys a better produced film but not necessarily a more unique production to watch.

One way or the other, *Black Caesar* is a great view into cinematic history and how *Zen Filmmaking* was working way back in the way back when. :-)

Shaking My Hand with a Glove On
20/November/2014 09:02

It is no secret that I love the unique finds that can be had at flea markets, swap meets, and thrift stores. I go to them whenever I have the chance. In some cases, I get to know the people that work at these locations; particularly thrift stores.

Now, shopping at these places can be a little messy. I mean a lot of the stuff you find has been in hibernation for a long-long time. So, I understand that the workers must be bombarded by the dust and the dirty day in and day out. Thus, they hope to protect themselves.

I was at a shop yesterday and one of the guys I know that works there sees me. He had been unloading a rack and stocking the shelves. He smiles, walks over to me, and extends his hand. I look down. He is wearing gloves to keep his hands from getting dirty. Keep his hands from getting dirty but wants to shake my hand with his dirty glove on...

I smile. I shake his gloved hand. He goes back to work. I recommence my viewing.

Luckily, I carry antibacterial gel in my pocket. :-)

Getting By Verses Getting Over

19/November/2014 07:49

In our modern society, which is full of Reality TV and the promises of greatness, we are so bombarded with the people that live the Life of Riley and are opulent in all that they do that it makes many of us believe that life is actually haveable. From this, many people walk the slow road to devastation by living beyond their means based upon the promises of a god of wealth that does not exist.

I know many people, since the economy has gone south, they have lost their jobs and have, in some cases, during their late middle life, moved back in with their aging parents. Sad. But, at least they have living parents. Others are not so lucky. ... And, when I say, *"Gone south,"* that is exactly the case. Due to cheaper rents, tax breaks, and the etc., many large companies have moved to the Southwest or Southern states, leaving their previous employees unemployed.

Even before the latest blast to the economy, which has taken places over the past six or seven years, I witnessed people being damned by the job market. I knew people who's wife and kid moved back to their parent's homebase in Sapporo while the husband tried to eke out a living here in L.A. – trying simply to save enough money to get back and visit them. Sad. Time passes and then it is gone.

It is not only here in the West, when I was spending much of my time in Japan, during the boom years of the 80s, Japan's economy grew vastly. The Japanese people were very proud, believing it would last forever. Having a deep background in the study of economic geography, I knew it would not as their was no infrastructure to maintain its existence. By that late 90s and into the twenty-first century you would see long lines of people in cities like Tokyo, living in cardboard boxes. Sad.

Like I have always said, if you are willing to do anything you can find a job. This is especially the case in a large urban center. The problem in this equation is twofold, however. First of all, large urban centers are also very expensive place to live; rents are high. And two, people define themselves as, *"I am this or I am that."* They have a job. They do their job. They are that job. Then, the job is gone and they do not want to step down to something they deem is lower than what they were previously doing. Thus, here we are, millions of people out of work with no life and little hope. Sad.

Some will claim that life is a projected reality. And, to a certain degree that is true. But, life is also the reality of reality. What you see is what you get. What you do will equal your outcome. And, though we can each dream that our life will be like the fabulous life of those on Reality TV who do nothing, yet make millions, it's probably not going to happen. So, what you are left with is doing what you're doing defined by the reality of your reality.

Can you be peaceful in the less? Can you become less? Can you remove yourself from how you define yourself? If you can say, *"Yes,"* to all of these, your life may be if not richer at least easier.

Gridlock

18/November/2014 13:39

I was cruising down Inglewood Ave., about to get on the 405 today, when I heard a few sirens coming and I noticed that off in the nearby distance there was some smoke pouring out of an industrial building. The fire engines drove by progressing towards the intersection where they needed to turn. As they got there, the cars that had gone through the intersection had stopped. They were frozen; nonmoving. The cars behind these forward automobiles had pulled righted up into them. So, the intersection was completely gridlocked. The forward cars were not going anywhere; the cars behind them could not back up as they stretched back into the distance. I could see the driver of the lead fire truck waving and yelling at the cars to get out of his way. But, there was no police support. No one moved an inch.

Finally, with no one moving, the two fire trucks backed up and processed to retrace their path, down the same lane they had arrived in. ...Trying to get to the fire via another pathway.

You know, this is not the first time I saw something like this happening. In the last Non-Narrative Zen Film I did, *A Space in the Time 2*, I filmed a scene where a fire truck was trying to get through a traffic jam in a construction zone in the LBC. Frozen by the sirens and the lights; nothing, no one would move. Finally, a construction worked got a few cars out of the way and waved the fire truck through via a construction lane.

This is all just so stupid and it really goes to show us the true level of human interactive understanding...

And, you wonder why the world is such a mess. :-(

People Don't Want to Know the Truth

18/November/2014 08:55

As I often jokingly state, *"People don't want to know the truth. They just want to believe what they want to believe."*

Think about it, how often to you research what you hear from another person, in the media, or online before you reach your conclusion about what is fact and what is fiction? For the most part people simply believe what they hear with no further thought or investigation. This is particularly the case when something drives your emotions.

Someone states something about someone or something and the way they say it really pisses you off. You hate the kind of behavior that they are describing. So, of course, you must hate the person or the subject the comment was made about.

In reality, that is a natural (initial) response. But, think about this, have you ever found out later that what someone said about someone or something was completely false? Did someone ever say something false about you?

This is the thing and what sets the True Person apart from all the rest of the world's population. The True Person does not simply hear and believe. Instead, they chart any statement to its source and then make their conclusions once all of the information has been accumulated, analyzed, and studied. They don't just simply hear and believe.

Who are you?

Let Me Apologize

17/November/2014 10:08

I attended an exhibition opening at an art gallery this past Saturday night in Santa Monica. When I was leaving I bumped into this person I know. I gave them a nod and was going to walk on but they came up to me. They said, *"I really want to apologize to you for what I did."* My response was, *"Thanks for the words, but unless you can replace what you destroyed your words mean nothing."*

Now, I am not going to go into the whole thing about what this individual did. It was one of those things that dominates the film game, where one person was trying to climb up the ladder by diminishing another person's achievements. The way that this person twisted the truth of reality killed a few deals for me and presented me in a less than truthful light. But, that's life.

More to the point is that, first of all, most people are so locked into themselves and what they hope to achieve that they do not care who they hurt in the process of achieving their desires. It is truly a big undertaking when someone can step up to the plate and apologize. Few will do that.

This being stated, if you are mindful enough to actually care about humanity and other people to the degree that you will apologize, what do your words mean if they are not followed up with actions? I mean, saying, *"I am sorry,"* is fine. But, (like in this situation), elements of my life were broken and my evolution disturbed by what someone else had done, not by anything I had done. No matter what their motivation was, that is just not right.

So, I believe we should all take a long look at our lives and view the people we have hurt whether consciously or not. Then, no matter our initially motivation for doing the damage we did, we should apologize, not through words, but by righting any wrong we have unleashed.

Publish or Perish

17/November/2014 08:58

There is this saying in the academic world, when you teach at a university, *"Publish or perish."* What this means is that you must continue to do research and get your findings published via reliable journals and publishing companies or you will not keep your professorship. It is the same in the world of fine art. There, the saying is, *"Show or go."* This concept is revolved around the same ideology that the professors must be good enough to get gallery showings or they will not be allowed to continue to teach. I believe these are important factors that have set a standard for the education of our society. And, they continue to be practiced to this day.

Since the dawning of the digital age, getting your creations, (whether they be writings or art) out there has become much easier than in times gone past. Getting it out there on your own dime, if you will. Meaning, you can get your writings published or your artwork shown on the internet or via digital media quite easily and inexpensively. And, that's great; a lot of people have done it. But, getting it out there on your own dime is not the same as having a publisher actually review, approve, and then publish your work – nor is getting your artwork out their on your own, (via the internet or at a pay-to-pay gallery), the same as having it accepted by a true gallery.

It is important to note that academic institutions still hold fast to the rules that your work must be found worthy and approved by knowledgeable others for you to be validated. No self-validation allowed.

This is an important factor to keep in mind when you research those who you are listening to. Art is art and that is a little bit different; that is all about feeling and personal aesthetics. But, when it comes to those who you allow to guide your life, you must be more careful. Therefore, you must question, who else, beside the person themselves, has approved their knowledge. And, I don't mean reviews on the internet – anybody can fake those. I believe you must question, are they truly validated by being published by respected journals and/or publishing companies? What authoritative source(s) has approved a person's creations? By searching out and finding a person who actually is truly validated you then remove one layer of the possibility of being scammed.

Save Yourself

16/November/2014 09:28

There was a great song by the *McAuley Schenker Group* titled, *"Save Yourself,"* that came out back in the late 80s. Though I was never really a big fan of the Hair Metal bands of the 80s, there was occasionally some fun music and, of course, some great musicianship that rose from that era. And, as the guitarist, Michael Schenker, had come to fame a decade before that era, so, in some ways, he crossed definitions. Anyway, check it out if you feel like it...

To the point... Have you been made aware of the fact about how most people are really out to save themselves? They will be your friend in good times, when what you are doing makes them happy or you are helping them, but then you do something that they do not like or if times get tough, and look out.

I think back to this one time I was in Hawaii with this sweet young lady. We were swimming in this one small lagoon. All of sudden a tidal surge rushes in and the place becomes like a swirling jacuzzi. For me it was fun. I loved it. My lady friend, not that great of a swimmer, was freaking out. I made my way over to her to help her out and tell her to simply relax, as that is all you have to do in situations like this in the water. When I got to her, the first thing she did was take her hand, put it on the top of my head, and literally push me under the swirling water to keep herself up. Me, being who I am, I thought this was hella funny and I knew the tidal surge would soon subside.

But, here is an ideal illustration of life. People save themselves.

Now certainly, there are people that will go out of their way to save others and save the world; putting their life second before that of others. I like to believe I am one of those people. But, most are kill or be kill.

We rarely encounter situation that can literally kill us during our lifetime. Most of life is defined by more of an emotionally/financially motivated mindset or the, *"I want to feel this way,"* attitude. So, it never gets as life or death as the occurrence previously described. But, the thing about life is, every element of what we do and what we are force to do or endure has the potential to truly define the next and the next and the next stage of our life. So, the small behavioral things that people do have the potential to really affect us farther down the line.

In life, we do not always have the choice of whom we hang with. Nor do we commonly know the true personality of a person until it is too late. So, in life, all we can is choose our associations when we can and be the best swimmer that we can be; remembering to relax when the swirling tidal surge of the ocean rushes in.

Courtesy, Selflessness, and the Quest for Humanity
14/November/2014 16:50

I had gotten into my car and was about to back out of a parking spot this morning. Just then, an elderly Japanese man comes up. His car was apparently parked next to mine. He stood behind his car, smiled, and waved me out – obviously to give me plenty of room. Very courteous. I smiled and waved and began to back out. I was about three quarters of the way out of my parking spot when a guy races up through the parking lot. He blasts his horn for the aging gentleman and me to get out of his way. I smile at the man standing there, shake my head, and pull back into my spot. Very selfish, very rude. The guy accelerates past us. I recommence my backing up and leave the parking lot.

I am sure situations like this have happened you. When it does, there are two things that can happen. One, you can do what I did. Or two, you can tell the guy to fuck off and continue to back up. With this, you have to be willing to fight, which I, of course, am. But, fighting for no reason, rarely serves a purpose. So, it is better to just play nice.

I actually saw two guys in a truck take the second approach today. I was in another parking lot, a bit later in the day. A city owned truck, driving in front of me, and I were proceeding through the lot. These two Latin guys in a truck step on the gas and quickly back out of their parking spot without looking. They almost hit the truck in front of me. Did they care? No. Even though they finally took notice of him, they just kept backing out, then put their truck in drive and moved forward. Selfish!

Everywhere we go in life we are confronted with those who are courteous and more often than not, those who are selfish. Who are you? How do you behave? Do you take the time to think about others before you do what you do? Or, do you simply think of yourself?

I think we all can agree it is better to be nice, to put others first – to relinquish our momentary desires before we damage the life-space of this world by being selfish. But, how often do you do it?

If you choose to be a conscious individual then you will think about others first at every stage of your life. If you do not, what does that make you: Courteous or Selfish? Who do you want to be? How do you want people to describe you?

I Am Nothing

14/November/2014 07:40

The entire purpose of, *"Being Spiritual,"* of walking on the Spiritual Path, whatever your Spiritual Path may be, is to lose yourself in the cosmic whole, to fall into communion with the divine. To do this, you must lose your sense of Self. Here is where the majority of the work's populous, who defines themselves as, *"Being Spiritual,"* miss the mark. Instead of losing themselves what they are all about is defining themselves. *"I am This," "I am a That," "I am at this level of obtainment,"* and so on.

True Spirituality is not a graded pathway, nor it is a video game where you rise to higher levels by your accomplishments. True Spirituality is about becoming nothing; no-thing. It is not, *"I am that."* It is, *"I am nothing."*

I'll Make You A Star

13/November/2014 14:41

When you're in the film game, especially here in L.A., a lot of crazy things go on. I often tell the stories... An interesting thing just happened that kind of points to the mind-space of man, woman, and humanity...

About a year ago I met this girl. She works at a shop I frequent and she has a really interesting look. Plus, she is pretty. I spoke with her whenever I went into the shop and she seemed really nice. A couple of months after meeting her I was about to go up on a new film and I thought about her as one of the leads when I was putting my cast together. So, I threw it out to her, *"Wanta be in a movie?"* I did the traditional stuff: gave her my card, told her to check me out, etc.

A week or so later, she said she didn't really see herself as an actress. Okay, I get it. As I always jokingly state when something like this occurs, I told her, *"When you write your autobiography don't forget to mention that you were offered a starring role in a film and you turned it down."* All that was what it was and I filmed the movie without her. No big deal...

I bumped into her today and she, in somewhat of a frantic mood, explained that she was at a friend's house over the weekend, for a little get together, and they were showing the *Zen Film, Max Hell Frog Warrior*. *"Oh my god,"* she exclaimed, *"I thought you were just trying to pick up on me."* I laughed. *"No, I was actually offering you a starring role in a film."*

You know, this is life. People project their preconceived notions onto all of the interactions and offers that come their way. Now, I must preface this with stating, there are a lot of bad things that happen here in Hollywood, and girls really need to be careful. So, I do understand.

This being said, I forever find it funny when people find out the truth about a person's motivations and they were actually nothing like what they expected. They were actually genuine and sincere. I know that is a rare thing.

So, here's an ideal example of how people are offered an opportunity, turn it down, and later regret it. Thus, they lose a chance at the next evolution in life. I know I've passed up mine...

Overall, life is a strange beast. Sometimes it makes me smile. :-)

From an intellectual standpoint I understand but…

13/November/2014 09:39

We base our lives around two factors. The first is what we understand from an intellectual standpoint. Meaning, we are each taught how to behave, what is acceptable behavior, and what should or should not be done. From this, we move forward though life. The second factor is emotions. Here, we see life and react to it purely by the way we feel. Certainly, each person possesses both of these components for life interaction, but each of us veers more towards one or the other.

The person who follows the intellectual path is commonly more considerate of others. This is because of the fact that they are very much aware of all that they do; contemplating their actions. Thus, they take others into consideration before they take any actions. The person who bases their life upon emotions, takes more of the devil may care attitude and rarely takes other people into consideration before they do what they do.

For the most part, people do not choose what mindset they will follow in life. They are indoctrinated into what is acceptable life behavior early in their days, then they move forward. This is not to say that people cannot change. But, the fact is, most people never change. They are who they are and everyone else be damned.

Neither one of these defining emotional patterns are right or wrong. They are only right or wrong when other people are affected by the person who possesses them. This is the point where life gets complicated.

For example, someone may be doing something that truly damages your life. Thus, you study those actions, ponder their inception, and conclude that, from an intellectual standpoint, you understand what that person is doing. It is damaging your life but you understand. That doesn't make it feel okay, but you understand.

On the other side of the coin, emotions are an entirely different ballgame. Emotions are all about feelings. This makes me feel good. I want to do or say that. If you don't like, who cares.

This is a slippery life slope, however. For it is from this mindset that a person develops their detractors. This is because of the fact that this mindset is all about Self, it is all based in Ego. It is all about being inconsiderate and non-caring. Which, from an intellectual standpoint, is never good. But, from an emotional standpoint, what the person is doing is making them feel good; so all intellectualism is lost.

No doubt, each of us has been lost in the emotions of our moment and have done irrational, non-caring things at various points in our life. This may have been in the company of friends or it may have simply been when we were invigorated by something or someone driving us to feel very good. What we are left with, once these emotions subside, is the results of any actions we performed during this period of emotional elation. In many cases, we are not made aware of any damage caused, (if there even was any), so we move forward though our life simply possessing a happy memory. In other cases, the damage caused is brought to our attention. And, this may occur in many-many ways. Then what? Does it give us pause to correct or feel bad about what we have done, or does it make us angry that someone else is telling us not to have fun. Again, the individual mental response goes to the sourcepoint of who we are. Each personality will react differently.

In each of our lives we are constantly being impacted by the actions of those around us. During some periods, life goes along without a hitch. In other periods we are truly damned by what others are doing to our lives. But, there is little that can be done, as people will be people.

We each need to continually reflect on who we are. The simple fact of life is, we should never be so uncaring and unthinking to cause the need for our negative behavior to be brought to our attention by someone else. And, that is perhaps the most important element to keep in mind. You are going to be who you are and that is a fact. But, be who you are without overtaking the life space of anyone else and who you are will be allowed to exist without unnecessary karma or conflict.

Pushing the Cart

12/November/2014 14:03

When Starbucks opened it first store in Redondo Beach in the early 1990s, one evening I noticed a lady, maybe in her fifties, standing in line and ordering a drink. She looked frumpled but not homeless. As time when on I saw her there a few more times. As time went on a little bit further I would see her sitting on bus benches around the area, looking more and more disheveled. Now, whenever I see her, as I did today, she is pushing a shopping cart, filled with a bunch of junk, down the streets near the beach. I don't believe she is homeless, because the city police don't allow that in Redondo, but she looks in serious disarray.

There is another guy who walks around the South Bay area of L.A. I saw him today too. He always wears a white tee-shirt and white denim pants. Depending on the day, they are in varying stages of clean. He has been doing this for years. He will be walking down the street, very fast, angrily talking to some unknown form. When he comes up to the stoplights, he stops. He's silence. The light turns green, he walks, and again he rages. Not homeless, I do not believe, just lost in some abstract reality.

I think back to my uncle who spent much of his retirement years in Vegas. When he would come to L.A. I would ask him in the evening what he had done. *"I walked downtown."* What! That is miles from Hollywood. Sometimes he would tell me, he walked to Santa Monica. That's insane! That's miles upon miles. But, that was just who he was. That was his physical training, his workout. This in L.A., a city where nobody walks. But, when and if you do, there are a lot of interesting things to see.

My uncle was obviously very level headed. These other two people, not so much. Yet, they all walk.

I think to the spiritual tradition of Zen Buddhist zealots who take a step, then bow to the ground, get up, take another step, and bow again. They do this for miles upon miles as a spiritual practice. If you were to watch them and not understand their motivation you may think they are quite insane. Are they? I guess that is all how you look at it.

And, here's the thing about life. We all do what we. We are motived by whatever is in our mind. Something are seen to be acceptable and commonplace. Some are not. But, it is only us who holds the definition. Who is the say that the lady pushing her cart is not doing it for spiritual penance? Who is to say that they guy who walks and talks is not communicating to the spirit realm in some way only he can understand.

Get Out of Your Head

11/November/2014 08:38

It is really important, I believe, that people get out of their head. Meaning, you really need to get out into life and be interactive with people. The more time that you spend alone, the more you become locked into your own head; which causes all kinds of isolation issues, mental fatigue, psychological disassociation, false projections, and head tripping.

It is really simply to prove this to yourself. Say, for example, you are upset about someone or something; stay at home, by yourself, and that is all you will think about. But, go outside; meet and talk to people, and instantly you are infused with interactive energy and human contact. Smiles happen, life happens, you receive the energy of other people, and all of a sudden you are not burdened by what is bothering you.

Stop the separation. Go outside! :-)

Do They Comprehend?

11/November/2014 07:41

In each of our lives, certain people and a particular type of situation, brought about by these people, come define specific periods of our life. When we are surround by positive, productive, helpful people, then our time is well spent, full of achievement, and we are joyous. When we are interactive with the opposite type of person then our life is the adverse.

Some would say we choose the type of person who is in our lives. To a certain degree this is true. In other cases, however, we are forced into interaction with a specific person or persons. As we have no choice in the matter, they may cause our life to be defined by a less then ideal set of circumstances.

People are who they are. Perhaps better put, they choose to be who they are, defined by their own personality. It is essential to note, each person has the ultimate choice in defining who they are and how they behave. Many people do not choose to take control over their wild mind, however.

Some people you are around make you happy simply to be in their presence, others really bring you down. Who is to blame for either possibly? They are. For it is what they are doing and the things that they are doing that affect all of those around them.

Many times, when a person who you are forced to interact with is doing something that is negatively affecting your life, you question, *"How can a person even behave in this manner?" "How can they be so unconscious?"* They may be doing things that are rude, inconsiderate, deceitful, or simply flat-out wrong. The answer to this question is, *"That is who they are," "They are choosing to do what they do."*

Many of us, initially try to avoid the actions of those around us who are doing foolishly, unthinking, and unconscious things. We attempt to steer-clear of that person and ignore them. But, as time goes on, and their unconscious actions are continuous, we may be forced to alert them to their actions. From this, we hope, their performances will stop. Sometimes they do and sometimes they do not. Some people learn and grow from their mistakes; others are so locked into the badness permeating their own mind that they cannot. They continue their bad behavior, perhaps falsely justifying it to themselves – perhaps having other people who are on a similar path of negativity provide them with moral (or immoral) support for the road they are walking upon. In either case, the end result is the same, the damaging of other people's lives continues. Can anyone question the ultimate result of that?

At times, one has to ask, *"Do they comprehend?" "Do they not understanding that the way they are behaving is not healthy to the people in the world around them?"*

The response to that question goes to the source of personality as unconscious people lock themselves into a mindset of justification for their action and they do not care what effect they are having. This is wrong, yes. But, it is who some people are.

In life, it is not like a job. If you are the boss and a person is doing a bad job, you can fire them. They are gone. Life is much more complicated than that. Sometimes people who are causing you grief do not take the hint and go away. They remain, for whatever reason, in your life and continue to haunt you. This can be very-very damaging in the long term.

Each of our lives is defined by an enormous array of abstract circumstances. If we look to them we may be able to chart some of life's logic. In other cases, though we try and try, we cannot. All we can do is be the best we can be as we encounter all of the life circumstance we encounter and never be the person who does not care enough to care.

Roller Blade Seven: The Unseen Scenes

10/November/2014 17:36

As I discuss way more than I probably should, I am continually asked questions about and receive an insane amount of comments made about, *The Roller Blade Seven*.

That's All Good. I have stopped questioning why. And, I am happy to discuss the film even though it was created over twenty years ago.

It is one of those films that anyone who sees it will be set to questioning. I understand...

One thing I don't understand, however, for those of you out there in the wide-beyond of abstract Art-House filmmaking reality, is why no one sees the films that answer a lot of the questions about *The Roller Blade Seven*. Namely, *Interview* and especially, *Roller Blade Seven: The Unseen Scenes*.

Now, I am not trying to sell you a movie here. But, what I am telling you is that, particularly with, *Roller Blade Seven: The Unseen Scenes*, there is a lot of facts, never spoken information, and tons of unseen film footage in that documentary. So, for anyone who cares or anyone who really wants to know the truth behind RB7 – know more than the average viewer of *Cult Cinema*, you should really check that movie out.

Okay... I'll shut up now. Keep asking your questions... :-)

Different Rules Apply to the Gods

10/November/2014 08:28

I got the chance to watch the new documentary about Lance Armstrong last night, *Lance Armstrong: Stop at Nothing.* First of all, I am not a fan of *Slam Cinema,* nor am I a fan of Negative Journalism, or Internet Bashing – because the person being bashed doesn't have the opportunity to defend himself or herself. And, that is what this documentary was geared towards, to slam Lance Armstrong, his use of performance enhancing drugs, and his overall projection of Self.

In our society where everyone uses everything to make themselves better at something: everything from beta-blockers, mood stabilizers, Viagra, and onwards, I often question why this is/was such an issue. Do any of us believe that Schwarzenegger didn't use steroids to get to the level of enchantment that he possessed during his days in completion? No. But, nobody thinks twice about it. Yet, everyone seems to deny it. And, I guess, this is where the problem arises.

I remember when Hulk Hogan went on *The Arsenio Hall Show* back in the early '90s after Lyle Alzado stated that Hulk had used steroids. He denied he had ever touched enhancing steroids. Many years later, Hulk confirmed that he had, in fact, used them. So, there you go. Again, to the point, everybody takes stuff to make themselves better and in many cases they lie about it.

I grew up at a time when people where using all kinds of substances to enhance their mental and spiritual perceptions. Me too. Was it wrong? Some would say that it was. But no, I don't think so. It was simply a definition of an era.

In the documentary about Armstrong, (and I grabbed the title of this piece from something said by one of the interviewees), it appears that due to his success that is where Armstrong fell short. He became full of himself and the things he could do with the power and money he had. He apparently felt he could make people do what he wanted and if they didn't, look out.

Okay... Nothing new there... That is one of the subtle catches of anyone who achieves success. Not good. But, it is commonly the way it is.

But, all this being said, no matter what helped him to gain his physical prowess, Armstrong was still the one to train insanely and ultimately win. Drugs will only take you so far. If you do not train like a mad man their effects will be minuscule at best.

But, here is the thing about life and how we must each study all of our actions. First of all, like I have long said, *"Never claim to be anything."* By not claiming anything you will not be compared to others. From this, you claim no title, you take no rewards, and your reputation will not fall into damnation if you are ever seen to falter.

Let's face it, we are all sinners. We have all done bad things. We all do bad things.

Few of us, however, are in a position to actually do as much good as Lance Armstrong did through his foundation. And, I also must state I really don't care one-way or the other about Lance Armstrong. But, did his taking of performance enhancing drugs hurt a sport or did it help a lot of people? That's always the question that will remain.

If you do something big, whether you do it righteously or not, a least try to do something good with the fruits of your labor. Then, at least, the karma that impacts you for any corners you cut to achieve what you achieved will be tempered by the good you did.

Using Guilt as a Motivational Tool

09/November/2014 13:30

In life, we all do things that can be considered wrong. What is wrong? Hurting someone or something.

Many people when they do something wrong, they do everything that they can to deny and/or make excuses for their actions. If the denial and excuses don't work, then they justify them, *"I did that because of this..."* Or, they may even attempted to make other people feel sorry for them, *"My life is so terrible now because I was caught doing that..."* But, any way you look at it the outcome is the same, there are a large percentage of individuals who actually take no responsibility for the damage that they cause and few try to fix what they have broken. Thus, it can be surmised that these people feel no guilt. This, however, is not a normal or healthy psychological mindset.

From a psychological standpoint, guilt is seen to be a negative emotion. Negative, if it comes to define a person's life. But, more than this simplistic explanation, guilt is a good thing if a person uses it to make changes within themselves, stop doing the activities that are harming other people and other things, and use it as a driving force to repair any damage they may have unleashed.

In our lives we are each going to do things that hurt other people. Some of these are conscious actions, which are simply flat out wrong, but other things we do may be unintentional. Whatever the causation, if we do not feel guilty for doing them or if we try to lie and deny to cover up our responsibility in them, then this makes us less than human.

Sometimes, we have the opportunity to tell a person who behaves in this manner of denial, *"You should be ashamed of yourself."* But, many times we do not. The fact is, if a person is denying and hiding from their actions, telling them this will probably have little effect, as they will simply lie and deny further.

For those of us who actually truly care about other people and this Life-Place, we never want to hurt anyone or anything. So, we constantly take the All and the Everything into consideration. This being said, there are times when we are going to do something wrong. When we do, this is when we, as a person with a normal human psychology, are going to feel guilt. This is the natural pattern of human emotion. We should never deny this emotion; we should consciously experience this guilt and use it to drive us forward to do all we can to fix any damage we may have unleashed.

People come and go in all of our lives. There are those we will never see again and, thus, repaying them personally for the damage we unleashed may be near impossible. This is not to say that we should not embrace the emotion of guilt in relation to our actions towards them, however. In fact, we should feel bad for what we have done, and if we cannot repay them personally, we should use the guilt as a tool to help all of those people that we can actually help.

In other cases, we are going to remain associated with a person we have hurt. Then, the guilt should motivate us to take direct action to repair any damage that we caused.

The main thing to keep in mind is though we may all want to dodge the bullet when we have done something that hurt a person or a thing, we should internally be more then that. We should own what we have done, feel guilty about it, and do all we can to express our sorrow at our action, vow to never do it again, and to fix all that is fixable.

If you don't feel guilt, you should really take a long hard look at yourself.

If you try to dodge your responsibly for negative actions you are responsible for, you should really take a long hard look at yourself.

If you hurt people or Life-Things intentionally, you should really take a long hard look at yourself.

If you break it, you bought it.

What is the Reality of Your Life?

09/November/2014 09:36

If I may paraphrase the *Tao Te Ching*, *"Three in ten are followers of life, three in ten are followers of death, and three in ten are simply passing from birth to death."*

If you put the numbers together, that makes nine. What is the tenth person doing?

People live their lives based on whatever weird mindset they may possess. They do what they do defined by the civilization they find themselves in.

Have you ever been in the middle of a war? Have you ever had to fight to survive moment to moment? Have you ever been in a fight where the other person is attempting to kill you? That is Pure Reality. In that reality nothing else matters but survival. That is the True Here, the True Now. Everything else, the mental masturbation that the philosophers dish out, is bullshit. For if you have not experienced that level of enhanced existence, you cannot truly understand life.

Thankfully, many people never encounter that level of Pure Reality. But, look around the world, look at the wrong side of the tracks in your own community; this type of Pure Reality goes on all the time. But, it is There; not Here.

It is essential to understand, however, that though it may not be affecting you; Right Here, Right Now, that is not to say that it will not. The essence of that destructive mindset is out there. It is an innate possibility in all human beings if they are guided in that direction. Thus, you have to always be prepared for it.

This being stated, the fact of life is that the only time you have the ability to think about the Bigger Whole, the Greater Good, and the Mind of Enlightenment is when you don't have to fight for survival. If you are lucky enough to be embracing the lifestyle of sustained substance then some minds shift to the expansion of consciousness. Thus, the tenth person.

But, here is the catch, and this is a big catch; people turn to philosophy, turn to religion, and turn to claiming to be a teacher of these philosophies and these religions to rise themselves up in the eyes of society, not to truly meet

Enlightenment or God Consciousness. They turn to these crutches because everyone needs something and in some cases, someone, to believe in. They believe if they can become this person then they will be filled with all of Emotional Fullness that is missing from their life. But, it is all based on a lie. They are not Whole. They are not Full. Or, they would not try to rise to pulpit.

Do you realize that the Kamikaze of Japan did what they did because they believed their emperor was a god? Was he? No. Thus, they killed and died for nothing. That is Pure Reality. And, that is just one example. We can and should all mourn the deaths caused by these people as we should mourn the deaths and injuries cause by other leaders and false profits but that mourning brings none of the dead back to life, nor does it removed the scars caused by war.

There are many in life, many of the people here, that are simply Wrong. They say and do bad things. At the top of this list are those who claim to be the leaders, the teachers, the vessels, the profits for it is by their command so many of the people of the world have been damaged.

How many spiritual teachers have been found out to be complete frauds, who were only attempting to gain money, power, sex, whatever? What they were not, was a true spiritual teacher. They were not the tenth person, though they claimed to be.

Look to life. Look to yourself. Look to what you are dong and why. You don't have to be the tenth person. In fact, you should not even try. For if you try to embrace the essence of the Whole, when you are not the Whole, then all that is left is a life lived unfulfilled based upon a projected falsehood. Simply be what and who you are. But, what you should never do is to claim to be that tenth person when you are not, nor should you take direction from someone else who is claiming that status. Think about the, Why, of your actions before you ever do anything – no matter who is telling you to do it. If you hurt anybody in any way, if anyone tells you to hurt anyone in any way, then that path is simply wrong. Thus, you can never be the tenth person.

Be nothing and the ALL comes to you.

Life, Information, and the Generalized 411
08/November/2014 08:25

Ever since the dawning of the credit age there have been companies that put together all kind of information about you, me, and everybody. The problem is, much of that information is not true.

For example, when you run my background some sources says that I lived in a city that I have never even visited. Other sources say I have a middle name. Nope, not me. NMN. And, that's just a couple of things.

All this being as it is, the most curious thing about all this supposedly confirmed information is that there is nothing that you can do to change it or correct it. Believe me, I have tried. Once it is out there it is out there. Wrong or Right, the Power's That Be drive the bus and they don't let anybody else onboard.

I think this says a lot about life. Not just modern life, but life in general.

...Words are spoken, tales are told, writings are written, people hear things and then somehow/someway it becomes recorded in some *Akashic Record* that no one has the keys to – no one has the ability to alter, correct, or change. Of course, we will all say this is not right. None-the-less it is what it is, a definition of our life. Wrong or Right that is who we are seen to be.

But, this is not only the gigantic nondescript corporate entities doing this. People do this all the time about other people. They make up falsehood and put them out there. Do they ever go away? Maybe or maybe not, I don't know? What I do know is that many people believe. ...As something is written or spoken, it must be true; right? Nope...

Has anyone ever made up a lie or presented a falsehood about you?

Is your information out there in the world of the great beyond true or false?

Lies and falsehoods don't change who we are. They simply change how we are perceived.

Let's all start right now. Stop the lying! Stop our selfish one-sided projection of reality about people, places, and things!

Stop spreading the falsehood! Research the truth. Find out the truth. Be the truth.

Change

07/November/2014 12:13

You can change if you want to change.

You can change if you need to change.

Change is necessary when you are not happy with your existence, when others are not happy with your actions, or when what you are doing is having a negative effect on yourself or those around you.

Not Very Bright

07/November/2014 07:32

Most people you meet in life you pay little attention to. It is the, *"Hi. Nice to meet you,"* and that is that. You give them little thought.

But then there are some people you meet that you find very attractive, very accomplished, or maybe you meet them and you immediately realize they are very intelligent. In these cases, you may give that person a little bit more thought but then your mind moves on.

Human interaction is like this. Unless you are forced to interact with a person on an on going basis, the memory of meeting them drifts to the winds of time.

Every now and then, however, you meet someone who is just *Not Very Bright*. Meaning, they do the most stupid things. This could be defined in any number of ways. Maybe they make the same mistake over and over again. Maybe they are just a zombie in life – oblivious to all that is going on around them. Some people, when they drive, they get behind the car in front of them and never change lanes, no matter how badly or how slow that lead car is driving. And, these are just a couple of examples. There are many more. I believe all you have to do is think about your life interactions for a moment and the type of person I am describing will come to mind; Not Very Bright.

Now, I am not saying these people are dumb. They can most probably read, write, and add two plus two. What I am saying is that they are just too lost in whatever lost mindset they possess to every step out of themselves and into life. They just make the same mistakes; do the same stupid things, over and over and over again. *Not Very Bright!*

Sometimes we meet this type of person, take note of their condition, and then move on. In other cases we are forced to interact with them. This forced interaction may make us want to scream, but our life's destiny defines us, we are trapped – trapped into an interactive relationship with them. This may take place at a job, in the confines of a family relationship, or them living close to where we live. But damn, time and time again we must encounter, interact with them, and have to listen to or interact with their bullshit.

Some people are very good at acceptance and understanding. They possess the, *"To each to their own,"* mentality. They can look, smile, carry on a conversation, and make no comments to the subject about how this person should change and readapt their life. Others, like me, are not sympathetic. When I have to deal with this type of person I just want to yell, *"Wake the fuck up!"*

You know, some people who are forced to deal with this type of person pass it off to the mentality of, *"I'm being tested."* But, I always wondered, *"Who's doing the testing and why do they care about the results?"* Ultimately, I believe, all we can do is simply pass these forced interactions, with this type of person, off to the nondescript, abstract bullshit that we each must encounter in our life. …Life, where we often times have to deal with stuff that we really don't want to.

I realize this isn't much of a philosophy nor is it the passing on of any deep knowledge about how to deal with people who are just *Not Very Bright.* This is simply an observation, letting you know that you are not the only one out there who has to content with stuff and with people that we all really wish were not a part of our life. :-)

Trolls, the Quest for Justice, and Lie and Lie Again
06/November/2014 08:39

    I believe that each of us have encountered people in our lives that we do not like. For the most part, there is a specific reason that we do not like that person – a reason based upon something they have done or something they have said. Okay, that seems pretty logical and fair... But then, there are the people that do not like someone for no particular reason or a reason that is not based in logic or fact. Here is where life definitions become blurred.

    If you have met a person and you don't like them, you have a reason. On the other hand, when you do not like a person that you do not personally know and have had no personal interaction with, you are basing your dislike on hearsay or simply misplaced emotions like jealousy or envy.

    I believe those of us who take the time to study why we feel a certain way about a certain person quickly come to look deeply within ourselves anytime we are feeling anything negative about a particular individual – we are in-tune enough with our own emotions to come to the definition of why we are feeling the way we are feeling and then, by realizing it is not a constructive emotion, put that emotion away and do not dwell or move any further through life with it. Thus, we are not bound or defined by misplaced emotions and our life does not progress forward constrained by any negative emotions or actions taken from those emotions.

    In times gone past, discussing disliking a person was left to personal conversations. You could say what you felt to your friends, let it out, and then move on to more important things in life. Today, so many people live their lives through the internet – driven by social and traditional media. They believe that the people they are hearing from and are communicating with are actually the person they claim to be and what they are saying is actually the truth. From this, all sense of true truth has been lost.

    Since time immemorial, people have sought contact. They have sought to associate with those of like mind. And, once found, that like-mindedness has caused people to move forward towards one desired end-goal. This is the same with people who seek love and/or physical companionship. Once upon a time people would go out into the real world and try to find a partner. Men looked for women, women looked for men, and that was the natural order of things. Though both of these scenarios are still the case; the world of seeking, belonging, and interaction has vastly changed. People still fanaticize about finding the person or persons they wish to associate with but now it is actualized in the altered state of the internet.

On the internet you must ask yourself, *"What master are you serving?" "Who are you communicating with?" "Is who you are associating with actually who and what they claim to be?"* And, *"Is what they are stating true or false?"*

In the realms of real life and certainly on the internet, where the world of illusion reigns supreme, people have a very common tendency and that tendency is to lie and deceive. People want to be more, (appear to be more than they actually are), and in the world of cyberspace they can be just that. No one is going to check your credentials if you are simply posting to a discussion board or are chatting online.

The problem with this, and to the point of this discussion, is that from this level of life-behavior the entire world has been set into the realms of believing everything when most things being stated are no longer anywhere near true. ...Things are simply being stated and because they are stated they are assumed to be factual. People then go on and on, saying this and stating that. They think this about whatever or whomever. But that whatever wasn't true in the first place so everything has become a mishmash of deception.

I was having a late lunch yesterday, (whole-wheat ramen), at one of my favorite haunts. TMZ Live was on the TV. TMZ is the ideal source of how a second of reality is captured and then a spin is put on it. It is then broadcast to the world as fact, when, in many cases, it is nowhere near fact.

I've said this before but I remember when Harvey Levin was an investigative news correspondent here in L.A. He did some great investigative reporting. But, then the allure of the dark side, probably based in money, eventually took hold. He emerged as an executive producer and later a host of television show(s) that go about bashing people. Sure, in some cases they are fun and entertaining. But, what they are based upon is, at best, a simplified and distorted sense of the truth. From what they air and the way they add discourse to it, they have hurt many people's lives. From this, others have rebroadcast and restated this not-entirely-factual information and much of the world has been set speaking of and on subjects, causing people to like or dislike, based on a completely altered sense of truth. And, I use TMZ simply as an example. There are many other sources of non-truth out there and some are way more expansive than TMZ.

Anyway, as I ate and watched TV, at the end of the TMZ Live episode it was when Harvey and Charles were reading their hate mail. Some of the attacks were pretty funny. One stated, *"You trolls... Blah, blah, blah..."* And, that's just it. In many cases that's exactly what they are, *"Trolls."* People embracing and spreading the negative for no good reason.

Today, we all exist in this realm of non-truth and non-reality. You can tell lies; spread the lies, tell a person, *"Fuck you,"* on the internet; speak behind their back. But, are you man enough to step up to them face-to-face and say it and then deal with the consequences? Most people are not. The world has now provided us with a forum for discourse and interaction based completely on this projected sense of, *"Real."* But, there is no, *"Real,"* left. At least not when you are living your life in cyberspace.

Real is here. Real is now. Real is living in this moment; person-to-person. Not projecting reality and being defined by the false reality projected by others out there on your TV or computer screen.

You like a person, you don't like a person: all good. But, you like or dislike based upon the truth of personal interaction, not an altered projected reality based upon lies.

Get Real! Stop spreading the lie(s). Be... Be who you are, what you are. By BEING you are not adding to the senseless chaos of the lies of life.

If I Can Help

05/November/2014 14:49

"If I can help, I will help."

"If I can make things better, I will make things better."

"If I can do something good, I will do something good."

These should be the mantras of your life. Are they?

Narcissism, Excuses, and the Path of Consciousness
04/November/2014 08:21

On the research tip, recently, I've been writing a few pieces for academic journals on narcissism and some of the methods about how narcissists deny and disguise their behavior in order to continue to get over on people.

With that as an introduction, (and I'm not going to get all scholarly with footnotes and stuff on you here), but it is a very clear human trait that virtually everyone sees the world through their own eyes, defines it by their own set of definitions, and wants what they want. Is that narcissism? No, that is simply the basis of human psychology. What is narcissistic, however, is when somebody does what they do without ever thinking about anyone else or the consequences they are inflicting onto others. Or, in the worst-case scenario, they do things that they knowingly understand will hurt the lives of others. Then, once they are busted or confronted about their actions they make excuses for them, deny them, and try to justify them. I am sure we have all encountered people like that. But, at the end of the day, what the narcissist has done is damage and/or interrupt the life of another person. The sad fact is, in the mind of a narcissist, they rarely are aware of what they are doing and most certainly don't care.

From each of our own personal perspectives, I am sure we will state that narcissism is unconscious, destructive behavior. This is especially the case when the narcissist hides and denies their actions.

If we look to the mind of a child, we see that they are driven forward wanting what they want and trying to obtain it. They may do this by crying or yelling. But, through life training and life lessons most children learn that this is incorrect behavior and not the way to consciously achieve their desired end. The narcissist, however, commonly never leaves behind the mindset of sheer selfishness and desire that is held by a child. Thus, throughout their adolescents and onto their adulthood they find ways to yell, scream, manipulate, lie, and deceive in order to get their desired ends. Not good.

The fact is, this is life. The more people we interact with and the more people we are forced to interact with there is, no doubt, that we are going to encounter a narcissist. It has been estimate that approximately seven percent of the world's population can be diagnosed with narcissism. The problem with this, (and this is especially the case of people we are forced to interact with), is that they can really mess up our lives. To this end, we must strive to remove this type of person from or life if we can. But, in some cases, we cannot. I know I have had to work with, on a professional level, a couple of people who were quite narcissistic. There was no way but to put up the mental shields and do what I had to do, until the job was done.

The problem with narcissism is that there are usually other psychological disorders prevalent in the person who exhibits this type of behavior. From this, interaction with them becomes even more complicated.

From a personal perspective, there are times when I have had to deal with these people and I would have just preferred to kick their ass. But, my higher-self won out. From a metaphysical perspective: life is life. It is a nonstop plethora of peoples. From each of them we can learn. Learn how <u>not</u> to behave, if nothing else.

To some, it is the higher good to forgive people who have sinned against them. If that is your philosophy and it makes you more consciously interactive with a peaceful state of mind then that is exactly what you should be doing. What I have discovered, however, is that many people who claim forgiveness, as a tool, are really simply burying their true inner emotions about the actions taken towards them by another person. Hiding them, instead of expressing them. And, as we all understand, that is never good.

We each, at times, want what we want and are unhappy when we do not receive it. But, we must always keep in mind that this is a divine melodrama and instead of losing our peace when things are not going our way, we can use these times as a tool to guide us to try harder and to do more.

As I previously stated, most of us have, no doubt, been hurt or damaged by the unconscious actions of another person. Most often, these actions were unleashed from a very selfish state of mind. We, as people on the path of consciousness, must always be more than that, however. We must think of others first. Think of the greater whole and the greater good before we ever walk down a path of selfishness, ego, desire, or believing, in any way, that we are anything more than anyone else.

Think about others/care about others, first. This is the ultimate cure for narcissism.

The Inspirations Are Out There

04/November/2014 08:06

Each of us is influenced by all the things that are taking place around us. Whether these things are good or bad, positive or negative, they are going to shape our thinking and our doing.

When good things happened to us, we are happy. When we meet and interact with nice people, we are invigorated and content. When bad things happen to us, we are upset. When bad or negative people come into our sphere of existence, we become discontent and angry. When people do bad things to us, we oftentimes react.

This is life. This is human existence. That is simply the way it is.

But, more than simply allowing the life around us, that in many cases we have no control over, to dominate our emotions, we can use that STUFF out there to motivate us and use it as a means of creativity.

I know a few screenwriters who have stated that whenever something upsetting happens to them they integrate that happening into one of their screenplays. Good idea. Certainly poets, songwriters, novelists use their life experiences to guide them in their literary creations. I do it too. I also use the good, the bad, and the ugly in my life to motivate me to write things like this. Some of these essays end up as chapters in books or at least the basis of a chapter.

The thing is, it is essential to not simply let the momentary emotions that come and go in life be the end-all onto themselves. For each of us when we are happy we fall into a space of harmony. When we are upset, that has the potential to lead to a lot of negative things both in terms of heath and ongoing life experiences.

People are going to be unconscious and uncaring in your life. You car is going to break down. Your computer is going to freeze up. Good things are also going to happen. You may find love. You be given a great gift. All of these can be an inspiration for you to make them something more than the momentary emotional experience that they are.

Use the Life-Stuff and make good things from it.

Fight Every Day

04/November/2014 08:02

For martial artists, (like myself), or boxers, wrestlers, or other people who practice the fighting arts, we fight every day. This is not to say that we go toe-to-toe, kill or be killed, but what we do is to delve into the subtle science of our fighting arts during everyday of our existence.

Myself, I have been doing the martial arts for fifty years now. That's a long time. Though I certainly understand all of the foundational elements and techniques of my style of martial arts, I never close my mind to new ideas and different understandings. This is one of the great things that took place during the mid twentieth century. People like Chuck Norris and Bruce Lee ushered in the mindset of blending the arts. From this, no longer was a martial artist only allowed to work within one very regimented set of techniques. Instead, a practitioner could expand their mind and learn from all systems.

But, more than simply viewing and/or academically studying the techniques developed by a wide variety of styles, the more a martial artists practices these varying techniques, the deeper their understanding grows. Even for someone like me who has been at it for five decades, there are still moments of realization either through teaching, witnessing the movements of other practitioners, or going hand-to-hand on the mat. As long as you keep your mind open, you can learn.

And, this is thing about life... Many people have their mind made up. Many, by the time they are a young adult, believe that they know what they need to know and never do anything to expand their realms of understanding or of human consciousness. Thus, they become stuck.

"*Stuck,*" is just as it sounds. If you allow yourself to become stuck, at any level of life, you miss all the great learning that is out there to be had. If you decide you already know everything, then there is nothing. There is only what is already in your stubborn mind.

From a martial arts perspective, these are the people who loose the fight. They go in with a very prescribed set of techniques that they will not considering altering or allowing to evolve. Thus, when they encounter an individual who is better versed, in a wider variety of techniques, they do not posses the defensive understanding of how to deal with this person's onslaught. Be more than that. Be open to the new. Be open to change. From this, life becomes a never-ending learning experience.

Survivorman and the Search for Bigfoot

03/November/2014 13:35

If you ever watched the show, *Survivorman,* with Les Stroud, you realize that guy is pretty hardcore. He goes out into the wilderness, for a week or more, and survives in some pretty intense environments. Good Show!

The other night I wish flipping channels and I came upon a show he did for the *Science Channel.* It was about his quest to find out the truth about Bigfoot. I won't go into what I think about the legend of Bigfoot but I will say, as all of his productions are, it was a very well photographed and produced television show. I guess part two of it will be on next week when we find out what Les finally discovers.

The reason I write this is that during the episode Les would go into long discourses about his past experiences with what he believed may have been Bigfoot and he also talks about strange occurrences like the way trees have fallen, forming a shape, and how others were broken in a very specific manner. He believed these happenings may have actually been orchestrated by Bigfoot.

During his discourses, I could not help but laugh. Everything he said, the way he described possibilities and circumstances, was so much like the way my character, Professor Andre' DuVena', spoke in the *Zen Film, Witch's Brew,* that it was scary.

Witch's Brew was one of the final films Donald G. Jackson and I collaborated on before he became too ill to film. He did his bit. I did mine. Of course, Don being Don, he never finished his part. So, several years after his passing, I put together his end of the footage and finished up the film. I believe that *Witch's Brew* is a great example of *Zen Filmmaking* though it is one of the *Zen Films* that has been virtually completely overlooked.

Anyway, it was like Les had taken his cue from that film and followed its evolution. (Though I would imagine he has never seen the film).

Anyway... It is simply funny how life and art parallel one another sometimes. And, how what was filmed, as a farce, has now become cinematic pseudo science. I smile...

Brahmamuhurta

03/November/2014 08:20

The Sanskrit term, *"Brahmamuhurta,"* is loosely translated as, *"God's hours."* Though you can calculate this period exactly, in relation to when the sun will rise, it is most commonly defined as lasting between 4:30 to 6:00 AM.

Brahmamuhurta is understood to be the ideal time for meditation for this is the period when the world is most at rest. I've written a long discourse on *Bramamurta* in my book, *Yoga: A Spiritual Guidebook,* and you can find tons of information on it elsewhere.

For those who truly want to delve into the more refined aspects of true spirituality, *Brahmamuhurta* is their time. They rise early; cleanse themselves and the sit for *pranayama, hatha yoga,* meditation, various other forms of *sadhana,* and study. Throughout India this is when the dwellers of ashrams work to enhance their understanding of greater truth.

Okay, here we are in the Western world, we want to follow in this tradition but nobody cares anything about refined spirituality. All they care about is themselves. They want to wake up, eat their bacon and eggs, read their morning paper, shower, shave, put on makeup, and go outside and start up their car to get to wherever it is they need to go to make money so they can buy the things they desire. BAM, *Brahmamuhurta* is ruined.

There has long been the propagated fantasy that once you are in meditation nothing can shake you from it. Wrong! Noise always hinders meditation. And, who creates most of the noise in the world? People.

India, with is vast population, is certainly not perfect. There is a constant movement, both day and night. But, the ashrams are set up to protect against this, at least to a certain degree. And, I would suggest everyone go there and live at an ashram for a time. Believe me, if you think you are currently walking the spiritual path, your eyes will be widely opened and it may curb a lot of the mental nonsense you are living and believing.

This being said, in life, living in an ashram forever, for most people, is not ideal. But, for those who walk the spiritual path in the material world what can you do? Some are lucky; they live in a quiet place with quiet people around them. That's great and *Brahmamuhurta* can be actualized. Others of us live in the city and we are surround by noise and the people who create it. Then what?

First of all, we must look at the source. People do what they do; caring little about the impact they are having until that impact comes back to haunt them. They don't care about the pig that dies for their bacon. They don't care about the horrible conditions the chickens live in so they can eat their eggs and so on. They don't care until they get high cholesterol leading to a heart condition, cancer, or until they are knocking on death's door due to their lifestyle. Then, it is too late. Then, it is all about excuses. Then, it is all about blame. And, this is just one small example in the reality of AM doing. There are a lot more. But, it is essential to understand; these people are the source of their own karma and their own destiny. The doer is the instigator of karma. The doer is also the ultimate receiver of karma. Yet, spiritual city dwellers are damned by the doers. So, what can you do if you hope to embrace *Brahmamuhurta* and live in the city?

There is no one answer but the best one may be, be silent when you can find silence. Halt the noise and the noisemakers if you can but then try not to become angry when your silence is broken when you can't. Try to adapt and define from when and until you can delve into your *sadhana* and try to anticipate when it must end before it is forced to end at the hands and desires of the doers. Remember, you are the one that is embracing the silence, the true knowledge, they are the ones that are creating the negative karma in their noise; ultimately it will be they that pays the price while you fade into the space of ultimate knowledge.

Braggart

01/November/2014 16:09

    Don't you hate it when you meet someone new and all they talk about is themselves and all of the great things they have done. Sometimes, maybe you even know a person for a while and still all they talk about is themselves and how great they are. Who do they think they're fooling?

    You know, there is one really very simple fact of life, if you have done something great, you don't need to tell anyone about it because they already know.

    I mean let's think about it. Do you think the Dalai Lama goes around telling everybody that he's the reincarnation of The Buddha? No, he doesn't. So, if you're not the reincarnation of The Buddha, shut the fuck up.

    Here in L.A., when you meet new people, it is so common that all they do is run their mouths off about what they have accomplished and how great their last project was and their next project will be. And mostly, they speak their words very loudly, hoping that ALL will hear. From this, maybe someone will finally believe them.

    Yes, yes, this is L.A., a place where people are most-often very full of themselves or they wouldn't have moved here in the first place. ...The land of opportunity and promise. Whatever... But, all everyone does is to talk about themselves and try to make themselves sound great. You're not, okay! Shut up and actually do something.

Arrogance, Insecurity, and the Play For Power
01/November/2014 10:07

As I have long discussed, arrogance in people is most often based in their insecurity. Some people who exhibit this condition understand this. Most do not. As most people who present with the condition of arrogance are not truly in-tune with themselves. They are simply reactive.

But, why do people choose to behave in an arrogant manner in the first place? Because they want to be seen as something – something more than they actually are. Though they, in many cases, know, deep down inside, that they are not what they are pretending to be, none-the-less they live out the lie hoping that if others believe that they are this something more, they will somehow actually become it. They live the, *"Fake it, till you make it,"* syndrome.

Some people who present with arrogance are in some small way actually in the position of dominance. Whether this is based in physical prowess, financial more-ness, or otherwise, what results from this is an ongoing pathway of attempting dominance over others. And, this is what arrogance is motivated by, the need to feel (and act) superior to others.

We all understand this is not a good fame of mind, but we each encounter people who are dominated by a mindset of arrogance in our life. Are you one of them?

Most people live their life. They are proud of what they accomplish, maybe even fight for what they believe, but they do not attempt to exhibit a mindset of arrogance. As arrogance is abstract. It is nothing and no-thing. It is an invalid state of mind, projected onto the world; pretending to be fact when it is fiction.

As we all sooner or later encounter an arrogant person, we must question what is the best way to deal with them. Certainly, the best way is to simply smile and walk away; never see them again. But, due to the fact that we all need to make a living, interact with people and family members we are forced to interact with, and so on, we may be forced into an ongoing interactive relationship with an arrogant person. To this end, it is you who must rise above the arrogance. Define it and see it for what it is – a distorted sense of self. Never let it control you.

From this, we each can witness and learn from one of the common conditions of human psychological makeup, based in negativity, held by many in this Life-Place and not let it drives us down the road to anger, frustration, and even violence.

Be more than the arrogant. Do not simply exist in the space of mental pretending and out of in-tuneness with who you truly are. Be something. Do something positive. And then, shun any rewards for your actions. Be whole in your self-awareness and self-silence.

Well-Adjusted Verses Well-Adapted
31/October/2014 22:23

I was sitting with a friend of mine today and we began to discus some of our mutual friends – talking about what was up with who. What very quickly became abundantly clear was that each of them, though some were and are very successful, were pretty messed up people, (from a psychological standpoint). As I was driving home, this conversation caused me to begin to reflect about the vast, wide spectrum of people I know. I came to the conclusion, *"Damn, we're all a mess!"* Certainly, I'm near the top of that list. :-)

Now, maybe this is simply the world I inhabit – that of creative people. And, as we all know, it has long been the suspicion that to be artistic you have to be a little weird. But, all this is just philosophy. What can it mean?

You know, I hear about well-adjusted people. ...People who had a good childhood and pass through life with minimal mental turmoil. But, I don't know any. Though there are varying degrees of psychological messed-up-ness among my entire crew of friends and associates, none could be described as well-adjusted. Each has their own unique demons. Sure, some of them are very successful. Some do the nine-to-five and have climbed up the corporate ladder. Some make a lot of bank in their field of creativity. Some are even helpers of others: cops, shrinks, teachers. But, behind the facade there is always a dark inner definition to each of them.

Do you know any well-adjusted people? Do they actually exist?

Open Your Eyes

31/October/2014 09:44

As a filmmaker, photographer, and instructor of both, I am often asked, *"What is the best way to compose a shot."* I have talked and written a lot on this subject and I think one of the main things you must keep in mind, (like I have long said), is that you must learn to see what the camera is seeing.

A camera does not see reality the way you see reality. And, each camera captures reality a bit differently.

I won't go into all of the technical reasons why, but each is different. The only way you can begin to understand how your camera views reality and how you can best use it to capture your vision of said reality is to practice with it.

With that as an initial basis of understanding, it must also be understood that a lot of times, with modern technology, you may not even be able to view what the lens of your camera is seeing. This is the case with both certain digital still cameras and the cameras that are designed to shoot video, as they only provide you with an LCD screen display to view your images instead of an actual view finder. Try shooting on a very sunny day and most likely all you will see is the screen and none of the information provided on it. Though the LCD screen is a great tool in controlled light, when you take it outside it is often times unusable. But, this is the modern world so you have to work within its definitions.

Many people when they go into a situation and know what they are going to shoot, all they end up trying to do is to capture the information – whether that information be a person's face, body, an external attraction, or in the case of filmmaking, human interaction. All they want is the information, plain and simple. But, more often than not, this information is static and boring.

From my perspective, what you truly need to do if you hope to create your own style in your photography or your cinematography is that you must open your eyes. You must never simply try to provide the information you need. Instead, you should integrate that information with your unique take on reality. To do this, take the time to study the environment, even if this is only for a moment. Integrate your subject(s) with the art that inhabits the space where you find yourself. And mostly, keep your eyes open all the time; actually look at and study the world around you, see what there is to see. If you witness something that moves you, photograph it. If you don't have a camera, simply witness the scene unfold.

If you want to understand how to best capture any image, always be a witness.

Can It Harm You If You Don't Believe?
31/October/2014 09:12

Many people believe in the power of suggestive energy. ...Energy that can be focused and then transmitted to a person. Wiccans, Witches, Black Magician, Sorcerers, and various other centralized groups practice with these energies.

Now, I must preface this with the fact that most people never even think twice about this style of focusing of energy. And, that's a good thing. Not thinking of it, their world is never defined by it. But, there are others of us, in the various traditions of metaphysics, which spend much of our lives investigating and defining how energy moves through the universe. Lord knows, I written tons-and-tons of words on the subject.

But, to the point; can focused energy affect you if you do not believe in it? Let's take a look...

Dion Fortune's book, *"Psychic Self-Defense,"* is without a doubt the most distributed book on the subject. The problem with that text, as I see it, is that it gets a little too deep into hocus-pocus and feeds the reader a lot of suggestive logic that only leads to paranoia. That is never a good thing.

This is certainly not the only book on the subject, however. An untold number of texts have been written: some good, some not so good. For example, The Rosicrucian Order, a group I have a certain interactiveness with has published a lot on the subject over the past couple of centuries. As have many others... Most, speak about how energy is all-pervasive and, as such, there are those who can control it and unleash it at will. But, is this factual?

One of my first interactions with focused or stored energy was when I was probably fourteen. This gay couple was moving from my apartment building in Hollywood to a building that was more gay friendly and they asked me help them move. I was happy to help. I was picking up and loading their stuff into their trailer. Behind one of their chest of drawers was a black tree branch. I picked it up, thinking nothing of it, but BAM I could sense the negative energy immediately. Later I was told that one of the men previously had been into Satan worship and Black Magic and that was his wand. Did I feel the energy? Yes, I did. Did it do anything to damn my life? No, I don't think so. I do know on my first trip to India, however, I did consciously wash my hands in the Ganges to purify any remaining energy from that touching interaction. But, just because I felt the energy does not mean that it harmed me.

So, is energy out there? Yes. Is it focusable? Yes. Can and/or do people try to send it in a certain person's direction? Probably. I have heard stories. Should you care? Why?

Here's the thing... If you go up and punch somebody in the face, they are probably going to bleed. That's reality. If you punch them a couple of more times, you will probably knock them out. That's as real as real gets. It's physical. It's here. It's now. There is no debate as to the cause or to the effect. But, everything that you can't see, is debatable. And, here is where you define your own reality. Do you choose to believe that somebody has the ability to have power over you? Yeah, I know, in all the movies and in all the novels, it is claimed that people do posses this power. But, that's just fiction. That is not truth. The only power that anyone has over you is the power that you allow them to have over you. Know this and the answer to the question is obvious.

No One Cares

31/October/2014 09:12

There is a simple truth of life, no one cares. No one cares how you are feeling, what you are feeling, or why you are feeling it. They care about what they are feeling. But you, no...

People have become very good at pretending, however. Certainly, everyone has an opinion about what should be happening and why it is not. But, what do they do about it? Some give to charities. But, that is the lazy man's way out. The way out of claiming to do something but in actuality doing nothing.

The ultimate truth of life is that it is all lived in the space of our mind – our own perception of life and of reality.

You live. You do what you do. You feel what you feel. You think what you think. You think of you. But, how often do you question what others are going through? If you do, what do YOU do about it?

There Is So Much You Could Have Done

30/October/2014 11:06

When I was teaching at *Santa Monica College* this beautiful Japanese girl took one of my classes on digital filmmaking. One evening I asked her about how she had come to the U.S. She explained that she had initially traveled here on a tourist visa, set up a business under a pseudonym, and then hired herself as an employee of that business when she returned to Japan. From this, she could stay here, with no expiration date, on a work visa.

OMG, I thought that was the greatest idea and it truly illustrated the creative ingenuity of some people.

Most people sit around and talk and talk. What does it equal? Nothing.

They may want to do something, they may wish they were something more, doing something else, they may even talk and talk about how special they are and what they are accomplishing, but what they are actually doing is that they are doing nothing, they just talk.

Some people even try to do something, but they do it in such a half assed, haphazard manner that all they end up doing is creating a mess in their own life and in the lives of those around them.

People are driven forward by their own inner nature. Some people want nothing from life -- they want to do nothing. Okay... That is very Zen. Others want to do something but in their doing, they do it all wrong because they either have no clear achievable end goal or they hurt people in their process of obtaining their desired end; thus their karma becomes a mess and little can be achieved with a messy karma.

Doing can only be done when it is done from a state of pure mind. Pure mind is a focused end goal for the betterment of all.

The girls I speak of, she came here with vision of moving animation forward. She achieved it. Thus, she served all, not only herself.

If your ego is upfront, all you will ultimately do is fail. Ego is the defining factor of that. Surrender your ego to the greater good and then the greater good can be achieved.

Shooting Star

29/October/2014 09:24

I was sitting out on my patio last night having a glass of the grape and looking at the moon reflecting on the ocean. Then, out of the corner of my eye, I see a shooting star.

Here in the L.A. it is pretty rare to see a shooting star. In the mountains, yes. In L.A., no. So that was pretty cool. The first thought that came to my mind was, *"Aren't I supposed to make a wish on it or something?"* But, I wasn't sure. This made me smile.

That's the thing about superstition; it is different in the mind of each person who allows themselves to believe in it and the way they pass its formulas onto others.

I know I've told this story somewhere, in some other piece of writing, but it goes straight to the heart of superstition, so let me tell it again.

My mother was a very superstitious and melodramatic person, as was her entire family. In 1967 her mother passed away. She was very old and that is the natural order of things. Apparently, at her funeral, it rained a little bit. To my mother, and her superstition, if it rains on a grave before it is filled up with dirt that means that someone else in the family is going to die within a year. Who made that one up?

Anyway, to my mother, in all her melodrama, she decided it was going to be her. So, for the next year, virtual everyday she kept reciting the mantra that she was going to die. This obviously messed with the mind of the young boy I was. One night, nearly a year after my grandmother's passing, my mother, father, and I were having dinner at a Chinese restaurant in the *Crenshaw District* of South L.A. We finished and got our fortune cookies. As I am sure you understand, for a kid that is the best part of eating at a Chinese restaurant. I opened mine, my father opened his, my mother opened hers, and there was no fortune in it. *"You see, I told you. I have no future,"* was her statement. My father said, *"Here, you can have mine."* He handed her the fortune from his fortune cookie. Less than a week later he died.

Whether my father's passing was instigated by all the energy my mother had conjured up by constantly evoking the spirit of death or if it was just the ongoing movement of life and death, no one will ever really know. I believe it was simply the chaos of life. But, that particular period of chaos was defined by my mother's superstition. And, due to her superstitions, if I was her, I would have felt very guilty. But, I don't believe she embraced that emotion. So, all that is left is the story.

This is the thing about mind, religion, and the promises of the promisors; they feed you all kinds of stuff in order to get your mind to play Mind Games. Some people love it. Some people thrive on it. Some people use it as a means to define their life. Some people use it as a method to conjure up all kinds of weird energies that are out there that we, as human beings, have no control over. But, what does it equal?

If no one had died within a year, like I am sure has occurred to millions upon millions of families who had a loved one pass away and it rained on their grave before it was sealed, then my mother could have just passed all her words and melodrama off to the definition that the particular superstition did not happen that time. Would it have made her stop being superstitions? No, probably not. Why? Because people seek something to believe in. This is where all of the nonsense of the world is born and how all of the charlatans, soothsayers, and religious leaders get paid. But, if we free ourselves from all of this Mind Junk then we are free, we exist in a space of mental freedom and purity. Then, all the charlatans, soothsayers, and religious leaders will have to go and get a real job and stop trying to make money off of the people who are simply trying to know.

Knowing there is nothing to know is the ultimate freedom. Be free.

References, Chaos, and the Game of Love or Hate

28/October/2014 08:40

I have always found it a curious process that when you apply for a job they ask you for a list of reference. ...People who will vouch for you and your goodness. Now, what does that mean? Of course, you are only going to give them a list of people who are going to say good things about you. So, how does this add anything to the process of finding out who is right or wrong for the position?

More than a decade ago I taught this seminar on filmmaking. It was right at the time when indie filmmaking, due to digital technology, was taking the world by storm. The seminar was highly attended and it went very well. The next day I received a fax (remember those?) supposedly from the head of the film department at a local college. He wanted to speak with me about teaching for his school. I called him a couple a times but each time was told he was not available. Strange, I thought. I called back until I realized that it was not the head of the department sending me the faxes at all, it was probably one of the students in the department, who liked my seminar and wanted to push me into teaching at the school. A recommendation? Or not?

A few years after this I received a somewhat snarky letter from a local university, telling me that they were staffed up and did not have a position for me as an instructor. Accompanying the letter (remember those?) was a copy of the letter I had supposedly sent them. The thing was, I never sent them a letter! I never asked for employment. Also in the envelope was a copy of my pseudo *Production Resume*, which looked like it came straight off of imdb.com, and my academic credentials. The problem was, the list of schools that were listed were totally wrong. So, again... A recommendation? Or not? And, how would something like this affect my life in the future if I ever actually apply to this university for employment? But, more than that, why does anybody bother wasting his or her time doing stuff like this?

But, I guess those people liked me... A recommendation?

The film industry is a very strange game, as is the academic world. Once upon a time, way back in the way back when, the whole reason I went to grad school was so I could teach. Then, I got my first position and OMG; the backstabbing that goes on among professors at universities and the subtle realms of bullshit is unbelievable. So, I left all that behind for a long time. Then, after making (some would say) way too many films, I decided to teach again. And, I discovered that there was still a lot of behind the scenes bullshit going on. Stuff that, unless you are there, you would never know about... But, I have the credential, and like everybody, we all need to make a living. So...

In the many years I've been in the film game and an instructor of said, I have met some great people and a few horrible people. One of my students turned out to be a great cameraman and became a great boon to several of my films. I would give him a glowing recommendation. Another of my students produced a couple of films with me; great/talented guy! Then there are the other students (and people in general) who have begged and begged for me to usher them into the film business. Me, being the person I am, always wanting to help, I showed them the ropes; let them get their hands dirty. In this process, some decided to hate me. This, after going far out of my way to help them in the first place. I doubt that they would give me a very good recommendation. But, then I wouldn't recommend them either. :-) But, that's just life... Especially life in the film game.

The problem with recommendations is that no one ever lists the people that hate them. But, here comes the kicker... You like or love a person because of the perceived nice or good things that they do for you. You dislike or hate a person because of the perceived nice or good things that they do for you. But, perception is based in your own personal level of reality; how you see and interact with the world. So, love or hate is all based in you. As such, the same actions performed makes one person happy and another person angry. Thus, where is the difference? The difference is in you.

So again, I don't know what recommendations mean? I've worked with people that other people hate. Me, I liked 'em. I've worked with people that other people revered. Me, I thought they were a jerk. So, the ball is all in your court. You see the world the way you see the world. You see people the way you see people. You judge the actions of people the way you judge the actions of people. The only defining factor is how your view(s) affects your life and the lives of the people whom you intact with and/or the entire world around you.

Who would give you a recommendation and why?

Yeah, It's Rare. But Nobody Wants It!
27/October/2014 09:50

When I was growing up there was what was known back then as a, *"Junk Store,"* not far from where I lived. It was on Hollywood Blvd., near Normandie Ave. As a kid, every now and then, I would go in there and look at the tons and tons of junk that lined the walls. When I was about sixteen, (many years later), I bought the one and only thing I ever purchased in that shop, a small cage to hold my pet iguana. Many-many years later I was driving by and I realized the shop was still in business. I parked and went it. Yup, still lined with junk and still the same owner/operator. Though age had caught up with him.

Times have changed, *"Junk Stores,"* have become, *"Boutiques."* Once looked down upon, they are now sought out. So, much so that pretty much everyone currently looks to find old cool objects in them. Me too.

What many do, that I do not, is that they seek out these objects to buy cheap and then resell them for a higher price. In fact, a medical doctor, who I met in my doctor's office and became friends with, actually goes around to *Thrift Stores* seeking out items to sell on eBay. He likes to go, *"Junking,"* as he calls it. I like his word!

I always thought this was so strange, however, an MD, the top of the food chain, and he goes and buys things to sell on eBay. *"It's fun,"* he would exclaim. I don't know...

Anyway, at the point eBay took over the world, everything changed in the realms of re-selling reality. The world became a seller's marketplace; especially in the early days of eBay. But, times and the economy have changed. Now, people may list things for absorbent prices but it is rare that they will sell them for that price. Yet, all the reseller always recites the same statement when you are trying to buy something from them, *"I saw it on eBay for..."*

Yesterday, I was at the *Torrance Antique Street Faire*. Interestingly, I came upon this vintage drum machine, made in Japan, in the late seventies. *"There's one on eBay right now for $380.00,"* stated the seller. My reply was, *"That guy's probably not going to get that price."* A vintage Roland Drum Machine, yes. But, not an off brand. Then I asked, *"Does it work?" "Well, I don't know. I haven't plugged it in..."* After some haggling, the guy said he would take $80.00 for it. Though I'm all about vintage drum machines, I passed.

Okay, here's the thing, the reason I write this, and a word to the wise. This drum machine was so obscure; it was probably this guy who put it on eBay so he could claim an initial asking price. Next, if a seller tells you they haven't plugged something in to check it out, that means that they have and it doesn't work. Who doesn't plug things in to check them out when you buy them?

Age and electronics do not mix. And, fixing vintage electronics, unless you already own the skills, is not easy, nor is it cheap. As such, I have been left with way too many vintage pieces of electronic art. So, my advice, it is best to just leave the unknown to the unknowns.

If you see desirable objects, (whatever your breed of desirable object is), you will desire them. But, be strong. Don't buy them unless you know they will change your life for the better and answer the needs you need fulfilled.

What Good Deed Have You Done Lately?
26/October/2014 08:28

There is the age old saying, *"No good deed goes unpunished,"* and I think we have all experienced that. I know I have. We go out of our way to do something good for a person and it totally backfires.

But, there is much more to the subject than just that. What if you don't try? Then, the person you could have helped is not helped and your life becomes all about selfishness.

But, more than just this, you have to forever ask yourself the question, *"What is motivating you to be doing what you are doing in the first place."* For there lies the ultimate secret to the riddle of what is or is not a good deed.

Let's look at a couple of examples. A week or two ago I was in the parking lot of *The Home Depot* and a lady comes up to me. You could see she had all this projected panic in her face. But, I'm a film director, okay... I know acting when I see it. The first thing I said as she approached was, *"I don't have any money."* And, that was true, as I virtually never carry cash. I said this as situations like this, in parking lots here in L.A., occur all the time – people coming up to you with a sob story and asking for money.

The thing about this woman was that you could see, once upon a time, she was probably very pretty. But now, due to smoking, drugs, drink, too much sun, whatever... She had a decidedly haggard look to her face.

In any case, she didn't want money, she wanted a ride. A ride... Normally, me, as a human being, would be happy to oblige. But, this same situation had happen to a person I know. A woman came up and asked him for a ride. As they were driving she proposed sex for a price. When he turned her down, she threw a fix, got the cops involved, and it all turned into a big mess. No thanks...

On the other side of the issue I have been walking down the street with a friend and when a homeless guy with a dog asked us for change my friend exclaimed, *"Why don't you eat your fucking dog."* Cold... Everybody needs a companion. Help asked for, but none given. Though it would have easily been given. Not good.

Those are both kind of extreme circumstances, as a backdrop, but the question still must be asked, *"What good deed have you done lately?"*

If you give a homeless drug or alcohol addict money are you really helping them? Is that a good deed? Probably not. As it is they who choose to walk down the path that landed them where they are. That is not to say there are not other ways you could help that person if you desired, but just getting them high is not an ideal resolution. Thus, not a good deed.

In extreme cases, of good deed doing, some people believe that they were chosen by god to spread his teaching and that is what they are giving to the world. Wrong! That is just ego. God doesn't choose anybody. People, via desire, choose themselves. People, via desire, choose other people.

On the other side of the issue, I have witnessed people who give and give; taking people out to lunch, dinner, paying their rent, you name it. It all looks like good deeds. But, whenever this occurred they had an ulterior motive. What they were actually doing was buying friends to fill the void in their life. Thus, their actions were based in desire and not pure in their application. Not a good deed.

From a more metaphysical perspective, selfless service has always been the call to action. *Karma Yoga,* as it is known in Hinduism. What this entails is that you do what you do with no thought of self. ...Doing, even if you don't like the doing. And, this is an interesting perspective to be operating from. And, it sounds good. The one flaw I have long seen in this system is that there is always an end-goal for the instigator of the action. They want something done and they want it done for free so they employee people who believe they are doing a good deed. And, I guess they are. But, at the root of the entire action is a desired end, thus any good karma is washed away as it was motivated by desire.

So, what can you do to actually do a good deed and hopefully make the world just a little bit better? Really, it all starts with you. What are you doing in life? What are you living in your life? And, how is what you are doing and living affecting the everything?

We each have desires; the what we want. How is the, *"What you want,"* helping or hurting the world around you? If it hurts anyone, it is not a good deed. If it helps, it is. Very Simple!

You can move up the ladder from there. Your lifestyle, your job, your recreation – are they hurting or helping? And, while you are doing those things are you hurting or helping those interactive with you?

As in all cases, life begins and ends with you. It is you and what you are doing that sets not only your generalized environment but also the rest of your life into motion. Do you care more about you and your momentary needs or can you turn them off long enough to do a good deed for someone else? It is a question you have to continually ask yourself because the answer to that question will define the rest of your life.

When They Just Don't Care

25/October/2014 17:08

I believe that many of us have had someone come into our lives that has just messed everything up in regard to our evolution, day-to-day existence, and overall well-being. In many cases, when someone is presented with the facts that they have hurt someone, they are very sorry for their actions, try to change so they will not hurt others, and go out of their way to try to repair what they have broken. In other cases, due to an individual's psychological make-up, they just deny any culpability and, in some cases, do not even care. This is where life gets complicated. Then what do you do? Your life has been injured and altered and the person who damaged it is not willing to try to repair what they instigated. How do you forgive a person like that?

Denial is perhaps the number one factor that not only keeps a person from individual growth but also from obtaining a higher state of mind and deeper understanding of life and the universe. But, look around you, even look at yourself, how many people do you know that live in an exaggerated state of denial? How many people do you know that when they hurt or damage someone or someone's life actually say they're sorry and try to undo what they have done? At best, most just try to hide from their evil doings.

Some people knowingly damage other people and other people's lives for the fun of it. But, this is a very small percentage. Most people do damage because they are either so self-involved with their own life and emotions that they do not think about the impact they are having on others or they simply are unaware of what they are doing due to living in a state of self-involved selfishness. In either case, the end result is the same and, as such, the motivating factor is virtually unimportant. Your life has been hurt and you are the one left dealing with the damage that was caused by someone else.

There are many things that people will tell you to do when you encounter one of these situations in your life. They tell you to learn from it, grow from it, use it as a means to gain a deeper understanding of human psychology, and so on. But, these are just word. Though they may momentarily help to bandage the injury, they do not change what has occurred. It is still you left dealing with the repercussions of someone else's actions.

There is no cure for this life condition for it goes on all around us. If it was not you being hurt it was someone else. This is not right, but this is the way it is.

We of a conscious mind try to protect and isolate ourselves from people who possess the negativity to injure our lives and the lives of others. But, they are everywhere. Sometimes we don't see them coming.

In the martial arts we understand that energy deflection is an ideal tool of initial self-defense. By never impacting force with force, you will not be injured in your defense. This understanding works at times. But, other times, your life is blindsided by the attack of this type of person and there is nothing that you can do about it but deal with what has been done.

Ultimately, all you can do is stay conscious. Be the best you can be. Never be the person who hurts another person's life. If you do, never deny it. Take responsibility and fix what you have broken. And, if your life is damaged by the actions of another, always be more than that person. Never let them drag you down to their level of limited existence. Because, often times, that is what the unconscious person will try to make you do, descend to their level of paralyzed mediocrity.

The damaging of other people's lives is the primary cause of why so many people are lost in the abyss of an unfulfilled life. They have hurt others. They live in denial of hurting others. They take no action in fixing the lives of those they have hurt. Thus, their life remains in a vortex of negativity which holds them back from any positive accomplishment they hope to achieve.

Be better. Be more. Do good things.

I Don't Care What You Believe

25/October/2014 09:40

Have you ever been walking down the street and a person comes up to you and tries to push their religion down your throat? That has happened to me in virtually every country I've ever been to. And, I've been to a lot.

Have you ever been at a party or a gathering and a person comes up to you and asks if you are a member of their religion and when you tell them that you are not they try argue with you about why you should be? That has happened to me more than a few times.

Have you ever been somewhere, minding your own business, and a person who is so full of themselves is broadcasting their religious and philosophic beliefs to the entire environment by talking very loudly, killing the atmosphere? Yup, that has happened to me, as well.

People are motivated by religion and what they believe. As it is such an essential subject to the lives of many people, when it is in them, they want to spread it all-around. They are right! You and everyone else must believe what they believe, or you and everyone else is wrong! That's their motivation but that does not give them the right to kill your realm of life and possibilities with their belief. Yet, that is what they oftentimes do.

There is something about religion and spiritual philosophy that answers a <u>need</u>. The <u>need</u> that many unfulfilled, unaware, unactualized people possess. And, it is easy. All you have to do is believe and then all your <u>needs</u> are met and all your questions answered. But, religion is like the illusionist who makes you think something is there when it is not. Where is it? Poof, it is gone.

The people that loudly broadcast are those who are trying to convince themselves that they believe. If they can get someone else to believe what they believe, what they are saying, then that gives them purpose and a sense of self. Again, all illusion.

In fact, in many religious and philosophic sects it is prescribed that the devotees go out and spread the message. This provides a person with both the individualized sense of self and the power of, *"I know," I am," "I know more than you."* And, *"Listen to me, I have something worth saying and you must hear it."*

If you are free and whole onto your-self, you never need anyone to listen to what you have to say. You do not live your life, based in a sense of insecurity. ...Insecurity, so much so, that you must go out and play pretend, while you try to convert others to believe in what you believe in. This, when what you are actually saying is, *"Believe in me," "Believe in what I have to say."* But, if this is what you need to make yourself whole, you will never be whole.

In really it comes down to one essential fact, if you are whole onto your-self, you do not need external guidance, offered at the hands of people who are only seeking self-gratification by speaking words that they do not truly understand. How can they understand when they do not even know their own true inner being?

Religion is an easy crutch. Religion is an easy pathway to <u>not</u> being Nothing (No-Thing). Religion gives you a Something. But if you are whole, you believe whatever it is you believe but you do not need to spread it to those who have no need to be lured into you over-exaggerate sense of unawareness.

In other words, I don't care what you believe.

Spiritualism

24/October/2014 16:34

Many people are under the false assumption that Spiritualism in America goes back to its inception. Historically this is incorrect. Certainly, organized religion was a very prevalent part of Western Culture, both in America and Europe, since time immemorial, but Spiritualism was not.

When I use the term, *"Spiritualism,"* I am referring to the belief that certain people can communicate with the dead, channel their sprits from the beyond, and speak on behalf of angels and demons. To channel these beings the process of conducting a séance or going into a trance is the commonly used tool.

With this as the description, it must be understood that this belief system was not prevalent until the mid-to-late nineteenth century in America. Prior to this, it would have been considered blasphemy to even mention the thought of conjuring up the sprit of a departed soul, as this practice is against all the doctrines of the Judeo/Christian tradition.

During the mid-nineteenth century, however, several things occurred that set the practice of Spiritualism in America into motion. Certainly, one of the biggest events was the Civil War. At this juncture of history thousands of husbands, fathers, sons, and male family members went away and were never heard from again. This gave rise to the charlatans who offered a pathway to communicate with the dearly departed.

It was during this point in U.S. history that Spiritualism took hold. It was usher in at the hands of people like Wiliam and Horatio Eddy, Helena Petrovna Blavatsky, (Madam Blavatsky), Charles Webster Leadbeater, Edgar Cayce, Florence Cook, Violet Mary Firth, (Dion Fortune), and to a lessor degree even by the Tibetan Scholar, Walter Evans-Wentz. These individuals were influenced by people such as one of the first authors on the subject, George Lyttelton who composed the book, *"Communication With the Other Side,"* and then combined this information with the emerging understandings that were arising from Asia, and the Near and Middle East on Buddhism, Hinduism, and other ancient spiritual traditions, including that of the Native Americans. Spiritualism was then glorified by people such as Aleister Crowley who lent a distinctively demonic edge to the belief system. From these early influences, in many cases fueled by prolific authorship, Spiritualism is now a commonly known element throughout American society.

From the beginning of Spiritualism forward, there have been those who have debunked individuals who claimed the ability to communicate with sprits and the dead. This factual practice has not, however, diminished its allure. People want to believe that their dead loved ones are still well and in existence out there in the great beyond, guiding and helping them. People want to believe that they are obtaining instruction from angels and celestial beings by someone who claims they can communicate with those on a higher realm.

Just as people are drawn to religion – seeking greater understanding about self, god, and the cosmos, some people are drawn to Spiritualists who they believe have powers that they personally do not possess. From a metaphysical perspective what all of this does is add to the ongoing ever-growing Mind Stuff that one must sift through if they ever hope to meet *Nirvana.* Mind Stuff is not only all of the desires, hopes, and dreams, that we hold onto as individuals but it is substantially effectuated by all the programming of religion we encounter throughout our lifetime and nonsense like the promises of Spiritualism.

Freedom is free. Knowledge is haveable. All you have to do is open up to it.

No one has any power(s) that you do not. If the dearly departed or an angle or a demon wanted to communicate with you, don't you think that they would? Why do you have to go to someone and pay him or her to get fabricated knowledge? Think about it...

If I can shift to a lighter tone now... It is like this one African-American comedian I once heard say, *"Why is it only white people get abducted by aliens? Why don't those aliens ever come to the hood?"* If aliens were actually visiting planet earth they would be everywhere.

Or, like the Hershel Walker character said on the TV series, *The Walking Dead, "I can't profess to understand God's plan, Christ promised the resurrection of the dead. I just thought he had something a little different in mind."*

In closing, studying history, religious and otherwise, and the mind of man (and woman) is an interesting subject. But, if you want to be free, mentally and spiritually, don't buy into the bullshit. And, when I say, *"Buy"* I mean, *"Buy."* As those who claim these abilities always charge a price.

Nirvana is free. What price do you want to pay?

Thinking About Others Before You Think About Yourself
23/October/2014 08:34

Life is a very selfish place. People, forever, think about themselves: how they feel, what they want, and what they want to do to you.

How do you interact with life? Do you think about others before you think about yourself? Or, do you think about yourself and your own momentarily reality first?

When you are yelling and screaming in anger, whom are you thinking about? Yourself and how you feel.

When you are in the throws of passions, whom are you thinking about? Yourself and how you feel.

When you are unhappy about your life being unfulfilled, whom are you thinking about? Yourself and how you feel.

When you are crying your eyes out due to your love having left you for the bad things that you did, whom are you thinking about? Yourself and how you feel.

When you are asking god or the cosmos for help, whom are you thinking about? Yourself and how you feel.

When you are doing *karma yoga* (going out of your way to something good for others), whom are you thinking about? Yourself and how you feel doing for someone else.

Life and human psychology is a complicated mess. But, there is one reality, people are selfish – they think about themselves first and you second.

It doesn't have to be this way, however. You can make the conscious choice to stop putting yourself first and care about others before you potentially damage their life by thinking first and foremost only about you. You can change the pattern. You can care. But, to do this, you have to care enough to care. Do you?

In the ultimate reality, this is the factor that will define your life. Did you only care about you or did you care about others?

Everybody Wants Everything For Free

23/October/2014 07:41

Every now and then somebody send me an interesting link to something that concerns me. Today a friend sent me a link where a person was on a board looking to download one of my books. The funny thing was he (or she) clearly stated that they wanted it for free. The responder sent the person a link to a site where I guess you can get it for free.

Now, I am not going to go into all the stuff about copyrights and how this type of action rips off the livelihood of the author and all that kinds of stuff, for I have written about all that many times in the past. All you really have to do is to think about what is right and what is wrong, how it would feel if it was you, and there you have your answer about righteousness, morality, and all that sort of junk.

All this being as it is, one of the byproducts of the internet is that everybody wants everything for free: music, movies, books, whatever… Because there is so much bootlegging going on and you can find pretty much everything for free. So, why pay?

As a creator, I have my point of view about this subject. And, as a creator I understand how other creators feel when they are removed from the equitation. But, more than that, owing something is owning something. When you buy something, then it becomes yours. This is why I so much prefer physical books to that of an eBook. Sure, it's the same information and you can store millions of eBooks on your tablet but it is just not the same in the world of touchy-feely.

You know, when you look to a bookshelf and you see books; there is something – something real and whole. When you read a page and then turn that page, that is living reality. When you look to a tablet or a laptop that you are just going to replace in a year or two, there is no sense of suchness.

But, to the person in quest of a specific book I authored… *"Thanks,"* I guess… But, if you want it that badly, I'd be happy to give you a copy. You don't have to ask the demons out there in cyberspace where to download it for free. :-)

You Ain't Young No More
22/October/2014 07:47

Starbucks is like a microcosm for the world.

As I have stated some six million times or more, I am a fan of *Starbucks*. Ever since it first hit L.A., when we were editing, *The Roller Blade Seven,* it has become one of my mainstays. Wherever I go in the world, I go to *Starbucks*.

Throughout these many years I have witnessed so many things at *Starbucks*. I have met people I liked who worked there. People I've had on-going relationships with. People I loved (literally). People I was intimate with (physically). People I put in my *Zen Films*. People who helped me produce my *Zen Films*. And, the list goes on and on... Mostly, my going there has provided me with many a microscope into life and how it operates.

...Watching the people I have come to know at *Starbucks* live their lives over time has been very revealing.

Recently, a manager at one of the *Starbucks* I frequent decided to quit, as he believed that his new district manger was going to fire him. He claimed the guy was out to get him because he was gay. Maybe... I don't know. What I do know is that there are always underlying stories to every tale told and everybody has their own take on reality. ...It's one of those things I will never truly know. And, that's okay. It's their business (karma) not mine.

In any case, this one employee, (a nice guy), that started his career at this one particular *Starbucks,* learned the rules, played the game, climbed up the ladder, and has now returned as the new manager. Good for him! Though I do imagine it is a little bitter sweet as it was the previous manager who mentored him.

To the point... There is this one guy who has worked at this *Starbucks* forever. More than ten years... Nice guy. Way back, in the way back when, he was very young. Now, not so much. In all the time that passed, he never played the game. He never climbed the ladder. And, is left here/now as simply a barista, while this other man, who came way after him, now runs the shop. It must be weird...

I have seen so many people come and go over the years at this one location. Some stay only for a moment, others for years. But, none as long as this one guy.

In times gone past, he was the young playboy, chatting up all the girls. I am sure that was one of the factors that lead to his long-term employment. I think back to when I used to run a booth at the *Renaissance Fair* for the *Sufi Order*. Believe me when I tell you, I understand the allure of being the central focus and all the acts of debauchery that it can lead to. But now, age has come upon this guy. Nice guy... Still chats up the young high school girls... But, it all looks so strange now.

And, this is the thing about life. We can attempt to hold onto youth; believing it will last forever. It does not. We can hold on to the mundane and the just getting by, but then time passes and what do we have to show for it? We can hold on to the belief that tomorrow will be better than today, but if we do nothing, nothing is done.

What I believe we all need to do is to never let go of the growing, the learning, the achieving, the evolving, the seeking of the betterment. For if we do not continue to try, all we are left with is the memories of our youth – a time that once was. And, we may be forced to survive at something we have done over and over again to no grand result.

Become more. As long as you do not hurt anyone in this process, all it can lead to is, The Better.

Keeping the Game Plan Clear

22/October/2014 07:45

If you ask a young person what they want to do with their life, many times they have very lofty goals. And, that is the time to pursuit them, when you are young. It is the time to go to college, pursue the arts, start a band, travel, attempted to do whatever it is you truly want to do, because time is on your side.

As you get older reality changes, however. There are bills to pay, responsibilities to address, and the grim reaper gets closer and closer with every day. With this fact of life, what you set your sights upon must be in accordance with your current reality. In other words, don't lie to yourself.

Many people with age under the belt develop or redevelop the desires of youth. They fall back into a mindset of, *"Then,"* and believe that is how they can still operate. It is not. It is unrealistic to believe this and it only hurts the evolution of the where you are now.

If you want to paint, you can paint. If you want to create art, you can create art. If you want to play music, you can play music. If you want to take photographs, you can take photographs. If you want to write, you can write. If you want to make movies, you can make movies. And, in this digital age you can readily get your work out there very easily. ...Very easily compared to how it used to be just a decade or so ago.

All this being said, if you are trying to make yourself something, at the later stages of your life that you are not already, it is nearly impossible. That is not to say you shouldn't do what it is you want to do. But, if you have the goal of superlative success, this will only hold you to the state of unfulfilled desire. And, this is the causation factor for unhappiness and depression.

It is essential to understand that the mistake many people make in life is that they believe life is only measured upon receiving the love and the acceptance of others. This is what sends so many people down the road of trying to accomplish something grand, in whatever field they are drawn to. But, remove that desire, that goal of great success from the equitation and you are free. You are then left to pursue whatever it is you desire with no strings attached. Thus, your life, no matter what your age, becomes free. It becomes an art form, as you are not dominated by the pursuit of worldly success. You are simply pursing the art or whatever it is you desire to spend your time doing…

Remember, a goal is a desire. Desire gives birth to more desire. Thus, a goal is never truly accomplished it is only the pathway to an unfulfilled life.

Same Old Lies

21/October/2014 13:29

I was at my studio today having a sit down with a young filmmaker. Thankfully, his project was going to be financed by his father. A lot of times people ask me for a meet, telling me that their project is all ready to go, but when we get together it turns out that all they are doing is looking for money. I DON'T DO THAT, OKAY!

Anyway, as we sat there talking all I could hear was the same old language. *"My film is going to be a big success. I'm going to get it into film festivals and from there major theatrical distribution."* And, the promises went on... The problem was and is, this young filmmaker was making the same mistakes made by so many first-time filmmakers before him. He is going to shoot a very contrived script. The seen it all before kind. He is casting actors that due to their names and the numerous low budget projects they have previously been in will kill any hope of wide distribution he has for his film.

Word to the wise, just because a person is a known actor does not mean that their name lends anything to a film project. I told him all this, but the young man was undaunted.

Now, I often speak about the number one rule of filmmaking that I discovered many years ago, *"Everybody lies."* But, it is more than that, *"Everybody believes."*

I cannot tell you how many young filmmakers I have watched walk down the same road as this young man and make exactly they same mistakes, while stating the same expected outcome. Some of them ended up bankrupted. Most ended up very disillusioned. Few finished their films.

On the other side of the issue, I have seen some young filmmakers who go out there and do everything right. They get down to business, (with money behind them or not). They get their piece of cinematic art created. They do PR and get their film out there. Most have not made any money on their films. But, they DID IT! And, that is the number one thing to be proud of. They didn't talk for hours upon hours about what they were going to do. THEY JUST DID IT!

As this is the thing... And, one of the main reasons I developed *Zen Filmmaking*... If you lock yourself into a desired dream, it is most likely never going to happen. If you lock yourself into a, *"Done a million times before,"* formula script, you are probably going to fail at achieving your vision for that screenplay. If you believe you can make a film that looks like it cost several million dollars for ten thousand dollars, expect to be disappointed.

The point is, and this is what I told the young man I met with today, *"Free yourself! Forget all the bullshit that you are telling yourself and the promises you are making to everyone else. Focus on cinematic art as you see it and get out there and create the best film you can make with what you have available to you."* Then, what will be will be. But, by following this prescription, what you will have actually created is your first calling card and the only thing that really matters in the filmmaking game, a completed film.

The First Thing To Do Is To Listen

20/October/2014 08:07

When you meet a person for the first time commonly what takes places is that they Over-Talk you. They are busy telling you all about themselves, what they like, what they dislike, what they think, how you should be doing things, and what they can do for you. Mostly, what they are trying to figure out is what you can do for them to make their existence more whole and complete. This type of behavior is based in two types of distinct psychological mindsets: that of insecurity or that of an over-exaggerated sense of self.

Ultimately, when you meet a person and they behave in this manner, this tells you a lot about the person. It lets you know how they see the world. They see it from the projected sense of self. ...As they are self-involved they want to overpower you with a sense of their beliefs.

Now, you can argue with this type of person; fighting to make your point known over theirs but all this leads to it the furthering of the constant chaos of life.

Thus, when you meet a person for the first time, the best thing to do is to listen; remain silence in your understanding(s) of life and of the cosmos. From this, you have the chance to peer into their personality and make the decision as to whether or not they are a person you should spend (or waste) your lifetime with or simply walk away from and ignore.

Destiny and Inspiration

19/October/2014 09:29

When I was about thirteen I found a book on macrobiotics in my local bookstore (remember those?)... It changed my thinking, (at least temporarily), on how to be a vegetarian. When I started *Hollywood High School* one of the first friends I met was a guy who parents ran a Macrobiotic Commune (actually it was big house with a lot of people of like mind living in it) right across the street from Ozzie and Harriet's house.

Okay that's the backstory...

During this period I found out about the movie *The Beatles* made called, *Magical Mystery Tour,* that had never been released in America. At the house there was this nice guy who owned and operated a movie theater on Wilshire Blvd., near MacArthur Park. I told him about the film, which sent him in the mode to eventually trade Ringo Starr some vintage movies he had for a copy of the film. He began playing ONLY *Magical Mystery Tour* at his theater for the next year or two. He made millions. It was the place to go. And, though he paid my friend and me some small change to pass out flyers in Westwood and help sell people popcorn behind the counter, we (me) never made anywhere close to the amount of money he made due to my idea.

He made his bank, moved out of the house, and sold the theater. Never saw him again.

The reason I tell this story is that recently I was in the neighbor and realized the theater was still there. Here's a photo.

Life, Ideas, Money, Who You Share Them With, and What Comes From Them... It makes you think...

Check the Source

17/October/2014 09:51

As an academic, historian, and published author on tons-and-tons of nonsense I can say with some sense of authority that you must check the source of your information, because a lot of stuff out there is both wrong and/or slanted to a very personalized perspective. Do you check the source or do you simply read it and believe it?

When we are young we want to believe. When we are young we want to be accepted in a group and many times that is defined by joining in with the crowd. If we like someone, are drawn to what he or she is doing, we join in the fold. We believe... And, perhaps that is the biggest fault of life and the biggest curse to humanity, (as has been proven throughout history), belief without the need to research the truth.

We all live by what we think and what we believe. But, where has the source of this belief arisen? That is always the question you have to ask yourself. *"Why do I believe what they say?"* From this simply thought, which will cause you to check the source, a whole new world of understanding will be given birth to and people will believe what is factually instead of simply something that someone suggests that you believe.

Don't let your belief system be based in personality. Let it be based in fact.

Over-Talk

16/October/2014 13:56

I went to my local Starbucks this morning to get my latte' and my bagel on. This Starbucks has a nice patio overlooking the ocean. I went to sit outside. Immediately, I hear these two ladies talking very-very loudly. The one was saying, *"He's forty-eight years old and he took me to this bar on Pier Avenue where he hangs out. Everybody there is like twenty-two. I was so embarrassed, everybody was looking at him like he was a complete loser because he's so old."* Then the conversation shifts to one of their friends. *"She's really not a nice person. I don't like her. The only thing good about her is that she lives in a bigger place than mine. She has a three bedroom, two bath and I only have a two bedroom, one bath."*

Now, I go to this Starbucks all the time. There are always people out there on the patio having conversations. Me too. I meet my friends there sometimes and we talk. But, what we don't do is Over-Talk. What these two women did, as amusing as their conversation was (in the department of weird) was to overpower the atmosphere.

Some people talk so loudly that they kill the entire environment of wherever they are. This is really a psychological abnormality. It is like they are trying to make themselves feel like they have a purpose – that they have something worth saying. ...No matter how trivial and/or negative the words they spout out may be, they scream them to the world; forcing people to hear what they have to say. But, nobody wants to hear. It's like the guy on the street corner with a bible in his hand, telling everyone they're sinners and the lord is coming and quoting scripture. Shut up!!!

It's the same with people who walk heavily – stomping across the floor. *"Here! Look at me! I am somebody! I am something!"*

I wonder if any of these people ever heard the old expression, *"Silence is golden?"* Because it is.

Don't Over-Talk. It just kills the environment.

H8 Watch

15/October/2014 17:32

For those of you who may not know, a H8 (Hate) Watch or H8 Screening is when a group of people get together, rent or buy a movie that they know is going to be bad, and then sit around; maybe smoke some weed, drink some ale, eat some chips and spend their time totally trashing the movie. Sounds like fun!

I've never been invited to one of those events but I know a few of my films have been the subject of them. I've heard from people who have H8 Watched *The Roller Blade Seven, Return of the Roller Blade Seven, Max Hell Frog Warrior, Samurai Johnny Frankenstein,* and *Samurai Vampire Bikes from Hell.* Good choices, I think.

Like they say, anyone can be a troll, a coward at a keyboard, and talk shit about movies, actors, and filmmakers on the internet. But, to actually plan an event and actually have fun trashing a movie with friends, now that is doing something.

Most of the time when we (me included) don't like the movie we are watching, we just turn it off. But, to plan to H8 the film, that changes everything. I have heard that some people have a crew that gets together once a month to have a H8 Watch. Good times...

I think most people believe that a filmmaker takes their projects very seriously and can't see the film's flaws and poke fun at himself or herself. For the most part, I guess that is true. But, that's not me. Yes, I try to make the best project I can with the limited resources at my disposal, but I never take my films seriously. And, believe me, any flaws you have seen in my work, I know is there because I watched the footage a lot of times, over-and-over again, while editing it.

I know what I'm doing. I have never set out to make Gone With the Wind, okay...

So, if you're ever having a H8 Watch on one of my films, feel free to invite me over. Believe me, I would have some stories to tell... :-)

If You're Going To Claim the Claim
Then You Better Be the Example

15/October/2014 15:13

It is no secret that the reason I am so down on all those who claim to be spiritual teachers (of whatever breed) is because they play the game of pretend. They are one thing when they are talking to people who don't really know them and then they are another thing when those people are not around.

Most people don't give two shits about spirituality. So, they don't think about it. Thus, they are not lured into the web of deceit that these modern proponents propagate. And, that's a good thing. But, as most of his have been indoctrinated into formalized religion in our youth, it is not hard to believe the promises of the lie. So, sometimes people get sucked in.

Me too. I was there. When I was young and first walking the spiritual path as a teenager, I believed. Luckily, I was allowed inside certain secret circles when I was very young and got to witness the process. The process of pretend.

But, bullshit is everywhere. I often discuss how at the beginning of any course on filmmaking that I teach, I detail that the number one rule of filmmaking is, *"Everybody lies."* But, it is much broader than that. People lie all the time. They pretend to be something they're not. They do it to GET. GET whatever they want. The fact is, unless it is proven to you, you cannot believe anyone.

Today, I was having breakfast and a guy was auditioning another guy for a position at the table behind me. First of all, don't go to auditions if the person who claims to own a big business does not have an office. Anyway… The prospective employee was hungry for a new job. The economy is shit right now so he obviously needed one. He listed his skill. The employer then went into his spiel, telling this guy all this bullshit about how much he would make via commissions and the like. He told him how he, himself, had just made a two hundred thousand dollar commission. Okay, all was as it was… They finished. Thank god! And, left… As I was leaving, I see the guy who was running the audition getting into his 1980s old, junky Toyota. Where's the two hundred grand?

This is the prime example. It is easy to talk the talk. The guy sounded very convincing. He had all the key words memorized. But, it was all a lie.

There is one truth. That truth is the truth of you. You know what you know. And you, and only you, know the true you. You are what you are. And, though you too may be one of those people who lie, deep down inside you cannot hide from the truth of you.

I can say, *"Don't lie. Don't play the game of pretend."* But, if you are going to do it, then you are going to do it. Does it make the world just a little bit worse if you behave in that manner? Yes, it does. But, I can't change you. Only you can be the true you. Only you can be the truth.

What are you going to do? What world are you going to create?

The number one thing I would recommend is to shut the fuck up and quit lying. Stop the game of pretend at its source.

Microcosm vs. Macrocosm

15/October/2014 13:39

Certainly, who and what you are surrounded by will cause you to think about certain things. Or, maybe better put, force you to think about certain things. …Commonly things you don't want to be thinking about… For me, I have been witness to all kinds of craziness going on around where I live over the past couple of years.

I guess it began about two years ago. Some rude and/or crazy people moved into my community and it all went to shit. Prior to that, this neighborhood was silent. During the day and especially at night you could hear a pin drop. No longer…

I've written about my rude neighbors and about the teenager who was beating his brother with a golf club because his brother had been beating up their mother maybe a year ago. So, there's no need to go into all of that again…

But, last night my lady and I were watching TV and we began to see all these flashing lights. We looked out the window and there were several ambulances, fire trucks, cops, and all the etcetera due to the fact that this one teenager had apparently slit his wrists. Sad for him as there's always a causation factor for that type of behavior – oftentimes the parents and/or their lack of caring or understanding is to blame. But, the area erupted with an array of lights. I would have filmed it but that would have been just too cruel.

A few weeks ago, the cops were over at that same residence once around seven in the PM and again at about two in the AM over the same kid doing drugs or something. Life…

It other words, my neighborhood has changed… And, not for the better.

I remember my neighborhoods going to shit around me and causing me all kinds of grief when I was young. Certainly, Southcentral was a violent mess. East Hollywood was no picnic. Violence and crime everywhere… But, here, now… It shouldn't be like this. I live in the High Rent District.

The truth be told, it is all based in the people who have arrived here after me. Now, the logical thing would be to move. But, this place has seemingly become like the Hotel California for me. You know, *"You can check out any time you like but you can never leave."* So, I'm kinda stuck.

I looked to my lady last night and said, "This neighborhood is going to shit." She said, *"No, it's not just here. It's the world. It's everywhere. Everything is going crazy."* Maybe...

There's all kinds of philosophy that I could conjure up about how to deal when the dealing gets tough. But, the reality is, that's all bullshit. All New-Age lies, excuses, and mumbo-jumbo. For reality is Here. Reality is Now. This is the life we are living. And yes, we can focus, get our shit together, and hopefully move up to a better world. But, in the process we have to deal with world we are currently trapped in and surround by. Our microcosm projects to our macrocosm just as our macrocosm defines our microcosm.

In life, we are either blessed or dammed by who we are surrounded by. But, the fact of the matter is, we can run but we can hide. People have the potential to enter our space and mess with our lives. That's just wrong. But that is the way it is.

Things Fade Away

15/October/2014 07:41

Yesterday I went over to my storage space. Whenever I go there, (which is probably the same with most people), it is a trip down memory lane. I was there looking for photographs I took in Northern Thailand for an upcoming book. As I was looking through them I found this photograph of a motorcycle I owned when I lived there. It was a pristine photograph of my shiny metallic blue motorcycle on a dirt road north of Chiang Mai. God, I have not thought about that motorcycle forever…

It made me remember back to this girl I spent time with when I lived in Bangkok. She had this souped-up VW bug with flames painted down the side. I always thought that was so strange.

The main thing all this made me think about is how virtually everyone I knew there (then) is now gone.

Drugs are insanely prevalent in South East Asia. Well, they are prevalent here too. But, the drug of choice over there is heroin or, *"Pong Kow,"* as it is called. Like a lot of young people they experiment with drugs and it comes to be the defining factor of many of their lives; leading to their death. Many of my Thai friends died from heroin (one way or the other). AIDS is also rampant in Thailand. People have died…

I sat there looking at the photograph of the then shinny new motorcycle. It is long gone… As are my friends and the people I loved.

This is life. Things and people come and go. All that is left is the memories. Then we are gone and there is nothing.

People Do Bad Things

14/October/2014 14:56

I believe most people do not desire to do bad things. They do not go out of their way to do things that will hurt, damage, or injure another person. Yes, many of us get angry, upset, or hurt by the actions of others but that does not send us down the road of intentionally doing something bad to the person who inflicted this injury. We walk a more civilized path.

There are some people, however, who do set about on the pathway of intentionally hurting others. Whether this is to physically injure them, emotionally damage them, put them in financial hardship, take from them, make them look foolish or something less than they actually are, and the list goes on.

Do you know people who have done this? Have You? I know that I have encountered people who have intentionally set out to hurt people. And, that is just wrong! But, there are many of these people out there.

In life, I believe that many of us have been hurt by someone who has intentionally set out to do us harm. Whether this infliction has been large or small, once it is done, in can never be undone and our lives are never the same. I even once had an extended family member decide to perform a very selfish and misguided action that really hurt my life. And, they did it knowingly and intentionally. Why? What did it prove? ... All it proved was to define the type of person that they truly were.

Why people do these type of things can be attributed to a million ideologies. But, whatever the justification, on the part of the person who unleashes these types of actions, the fact is, their logic is misguided and simply wrong. For if you intentionally set out to hurt, damage, take away from, or even take a person down a notch you are setting a world of negativity in motion. And, if you look to the lives of the people who unleash these actions, their lives are always the ones left to a constant chaos; shaped by unhappiness, repercussions, and tragedy.

There is nothing that we can do to stop people from doing bad things. If we could, these actions would have been halted millenniums ago. We can, however, keep our eyes open, look both ways before we cross the street, maintain a certain sense of conscious, realized paranoia about the possibilities of what a person has the potential of doing. But, there is no doubt, that sooner-or-latter we are each going to get sucker punched. Not right. But reality.

    Make the world a better place. Never do anything that will hurt anyone.

At Some Point
You Have To Stop Thinking About Yourself
13/October/2014 13:10

Human life is defined by two primary personalities, those who think about themselves and those who think about others. I guess we could label this the *Yin and Yang* of Human Temperament.

Just as in *The Theory of Yin and Yang*, there may be a small amount of the opposite in the dominant, yet each person is primarily subjugated by one of these two mindsets. Which one are you? Do you think about yourself first and foremost or do you think about others?

In life it is very easy to see those who think about others first. They give before they take. They are helpful. They are silent in the midst of chaos; never lending to the growing of anything bad or negative. They are quiet instead of being boisterous.

It is just as easy to define those who think about themselves first. They are loud, obnoxious, self-centered, self-involved, egocentric, dominant, pushy, and they lack awareness about those around them.

Parents are ideal microscopes into these two personalities. There are some parents who dominate their children or live their unfulfilled life fantasies through them; forcing them to be who they want them to be. Then, there are those parents who give, nurture, guide, and encourage. The ultimate outcome of the child that becomes the adult can be measured by how they were raised.

Life is a tricky place. You have to be careful about your legacy. For in the end, your legacy will be all that is left of your very limited life-time.

How do you want to be remembered? For having thought of yourself first, while messing with the live(s) of others? Or, for having sacrificed any momentary desire you may have had and having truly given?

The true definition of a person's life comes from what they have done to and for others, not by what they have done or accomplished for themselves.

Damned for Eternity

13/October/2014 07:35

In life we each encounter our own unique reality defined by what we are given through destiny and then what we decide to do with it. Each person is different. Though we may be sitting right next to a person born on the same day as us, and having grown up in the exact same setting, we are complete different people. From this, the complexities of life are given birth to.

Recently, I have been pushed into thinking and writing a lot about karma. The funny thing is, I forever attempt to avoid this subject, as it is such a complex ideology defined by individuality.

None-the-less, due to my foundations in the subject: as I have written a lot about it, had some academic papers published on the subject of how various religious traditions and society define and interact with karma, did a radio show on the subject a couple of weeks back, and not too long ago was even asked to write a book on the subject by this publishing company, based in India, that I have worked with a few times in the past. I tuned the offer down, however, as it is simply one of those subjects that invites heated personally motivated criticism – which is just such a waste of energy.

All this being said, a week or so ago one of my friends, who has been lamenting about some bad things he had done to this one person was telling me that he had been trying to do, as he put it, *"Good karma stuff,"* to make up for it. I questioned did he do anything for the person he hurt. *"I can't... I just can't,"* he answered. I joking responded, *"In that case, I guess you'll be damned for eternity."*

For what is karma if it is not fixing what you broke in one specific person's life? What is trying to fix your karma if you do not return to the source?

"Good karma stuff," is great for the big picture. But, it is the, *"Small karma stuff,"* that addresses your individual misdeeds.

Disturbing the Tranquility

10/October/2014 07:22

When people think of true tranquility they oftentimes think of nature. This is a clear thought. Nature is beautiful: the ocean, the mountains, the forest, the desert. But, nature can also be very turbulent. There are earthquakes, violent storms, tsunamis.

There is also conflict in nature. Most of us have seen animals battle on TV, if not in real life. One time I even saw two small birds going at it; kill or be killed. It was very sad.

All this being said, we as human beings desire a sense of peace and tranquility in our lives. We want the safety and solitude of a peaceful, quiet, natural environment. But, those around us often disrupt this desire. We too are all sinners. When we are or were young, many of us cranked up the music, believing that it meant something. We drive cars. We watch TV. We argue. And, the list goes on. But, past all that we are defined by the world we live in. That world is quite often anything but tranquil.

There are loud people, noisy neighbors, cars with alarms... Don't you hate that when you are sitting somewhere or walking by a car and all of sudden there is a loud honk from that car due to someone arming their alarm. Or how, out of nowhere, someone's car alarm goes off for no reason. How disruptive!

Then, there are the people who try to make noise. The, *"Hey, look over here at me,"* set. For example, I was having breakfast at this outdoor restaurant a few weeks ago and this middle-aged guy get on his Harley and reeves it up very loudly, to impress his friends, without even caring that there are people sitting right next to him. It was so loud that the lady sitting next to me put her hands of the ears of her puppy. What an asshole!

Then there are people like the newspaper delivery guys who drive around early in the morning, usually in junky, noisy pickup trucks, haphazardly throwing their newspaper, ultimately disturbing everyone. Who even reads the old school newspaper anymore? All that is bad for our environment and bad for tranquility. It's not like in Japan where the newspaper guy precisely delivers each one...

Our peace, our tranquility is damned by our environment, the people who inhabit our environment, their self-centered behavior, and, to whatever degree, by our own financial definitions. For, I suppose, with enough money you can buy a space, not defined by those around you. That would be nice...

Life is an interactive place. That's not bad. But, due to this fact, we are each defined by all those around us. That is bad...

Very sad... But, tranquility is hard to find and harder to hold on to.

Isolate the Moment

08/October/2014 08:17

For each of us, life gets pretty crappy sometimes. We are surround by a world we are not happy with and it feels like external forces are attacking us and we have no true way to defend ourselves. In these times, no self-help technique is going to make anything any better. We are trapped. And, though we, of course, try to chart our way out of this predicament, we are still locked in our prison.

In these times, you must look to the moments. And, there are always a few. Moments when, if even for a second, things are okay.

You must isolate those moments; appreciate them, relish in them. Turn the, all that's going on, off in your brain and just sit back and experience the niceness of whatever that moment brings, even if it only lasts for a second.

If you take the time to notice of these moments, then all of the bullshit you are living through may become a little bit more bearable.

Don't Force the Art

07/October/2014 09:42

Because I have made a long list of *Zen Films*, people often bring to my attention the artsy films made by others. Many of them are very good. Some... Well, they try to force the issue.

It is hard for me to see it or understand it but many people tell me that my films and my filmmaking philosophy have been an inspiration to them. *"Thank you,"* I guess... And, that's great. I am glad I could be of help in any small way.

But, there is a long list of indie filmmakers that I have noticed who really miss the point. They try to make their movies look bad. Bad, in the sense that they over do the doing. For example, I have seen many a film where they intentionally leave the lights in the shot, the actors try to act badly, they try to make their movie look like a crappy low budget production, and the list goes on... Or, they simply mimic the films that have come to be considered schlocky from the past, instead of creating their own wholeness; their own uniqueness of project and of style.

They say, *"Imitation is the greatest form of flattery."* All good... But, when you look to some of the works of someone like say, Warhol... Yes, he did things that could be seen as poor filmmaking technique in some of his Art House pieces, but he did it first. He did it to do it. Thus, he was undoing what was done. Not mimicking anyone.

Art is about making it your own. Art is about creating your own style. Certainly, in art and film art you can reference those who have come before you. But, there is no reason to make something intentionally look less.

If you want to do Art House do it. But, make it your own.

That's You. That's Not Me.

07/October/2014 09:21

Everybody in the world has a sense that everyone should be just like them. The way (you) are, is the way everyone should be. What you do, what you think, how you do what you do – that is right.

Think about it... Do you judge other people by how they behave?

When we are young we are easily influenced by the elements around us. What is in our culture, the press, the words of those we interact with, and so on. That is the place where we are formed. ...Formed by a combination of inborn personality and what we are lured into.

It is from that point that we emerge as who and what we are – how we see, interact with, and judge the world around us.

For each of us, we end up liking what we like and disliking what we don't like. We form friendships with those of similar, tolerable minds, and we shy away from those with a different set of precepts.

Life is like that...

The problem arises in the fact that we are not always allowed to choose all of those we interact with. In many cases we are forced to deal with people we wish we would have never even known. Again, life is like that...

These forced relationships can come to define a person's life. They can cause anger, unhappiness, depression, rising blood pressure, and the list goes on. They can also cause people to react and do bad – reactive, things. Which is never to anyone's advantage.

Ultimately, this is the game of life; we are all forced to play it. Though some may be able to remain more sheltered than others, we each have to play. We each have to interact.

All you can do is to keep moving through it as clearly and cleanly as possible. One can say, *"Accept all for who they are."* But, let's face facts, nobody can do that.

All you can do is stay as far away from the people you don't want to deal with and when you are forced to deal with them, remain mentally removed. Don't let the person they are, the person you do not like, control your moment.

Once Upon a Time

06/October/2014 19:20

I had a chance to watch the Sergio Leone film, *Once Upon Time in the West,* the other day. I first saw this film when it was released to the theaters when I was a young boy. I have since seen it a few other times in its entirety and, of course, pieces of it here and there on TV.

I am not a super big fan of the film. The storyline, character development, acting by several of the actors, and the looping all leave a lot to be desired. But, while watching it again there is one thing that was and is very clear, that film is the *Master Class on Cinematography* and how to construct the various visual images of a film. If you want to see how it should be done. Watch that movie.

As I sat there watching the climatic scene of the film where Charles Bronson's character kills Henry Fonda's character, I could not help but think, there it was the late 1960s, this film was released around the same time Henry Fonda's son, Peter Fonda had created *Easy Rider* in association with Dennis Hopper. ...*Easy Rider,* a film that defined a generation. Great time period for the Fondas.

As the film came to its conclusion, I also thought, pretty much everyone who made up the cast and crew of this movie is dead. Long gone but the movie still lives on. This is life. This is cinema.

Rising Human Consciousness

06/October/2014 19:15

I think that we – those of use who focus our lives upon rising human consciousness oftentimes forget that most of the world does not care. They could care less about the big picture, the evolution of humanity, or the betterment of the all. All they care about is themselves.

Most people never even think about the meaning of life until they are close to death. Then, they become religious. They fall back onto what they were programed into during their childhood. This is not bad or good, this is simply the way it is.

Now certainly… And, I talk about this over and over and over again, there are tons of people who use the broader term, *"Consciousness,"* to obtain their own desires. Whether it is to fulfill their psychological lacking, their desire for sex and money, or their desire for power – being the presenter of religion and consciousness is a great way to get what they want and hide it all under the guise of holiness.

The people who live at this level of reality seek out the seekers. …Those who want to understand more about rising consciousness. Then, they take them for a ride. Wrong, of course. But, very-very commonplace.

But, to the point and a word to the wise… We, (myself included), should never forget that most people do not care about the vision we see and what we are attempting to actualize – both in our lives and for the world around us. To them, we are just weird. And, that's okay. We are. We are, because we are different and not part of the masses that only care about themselves.

This being said, we have to be careful because it is a fine line between pursuing rising consciousness and ego gratification. It is a fine line to be with the people but not of the people. To be one with all but superior to none.

In life, those who choose the path of consciousness are choosing the hardest path because there are no hard and fast rules and there is never support from the majority.

Lingering Karma

06/October/2014 08:06

Did you think about you first or did you think about them?

Did you invade, take, use, break, steal to serve your own ends?

Did you hurt, damage, not think, not care?

When your life is being hurt, attacked, damaged, taken from are you upset?

Why do you do to others what you do not want done to you?

Here/Now is what you created with your life.

People Believe

06/October/2014 07:22

What do you believe in? Do you believe in a god, a religion, a higher truth? Whatever it is, that is what you believe. Yes, though time your understanding of what you believe may evolve. But, no matter how much it evolves, it is simply what you believe.

This is the same with everyone across they globe. Whatever the source or the causation factor, everybody believes in something. Maybe that something is a nothing. But, it is, none-the-less, what they believe.

Most people believe what they believe and understand that others believe in something else. But, because they believe in something, they believe that whatever someone else believes in is wrong. Most people are not all that fanatical in their belief system, however. They may think what another person believes is not right or not true but they let them alone, believing what they believe.

Then, there are those who make a life and make a living out of telling people what they should believe. Even if their voice is only based in criticisms of what others should or should not believe; this voice is one based in individualized belief.

Belief is just that, belief. Belief is not fact. Belief is not truth. Belief is only the fact and the truth that one individual believes. The person standing right next to you may have a completely different set of beliefs. This should give everyone the clue that we all are different and we should simply be allowed to believe in what we believe in. Throughout history, however, this has never been the case. People want to force their beliefs down the throat of others. They want to claim their belief is the only one based in fact.

Belief is never factual, no matter what its source. Belief is only an idea locked in the mind of an individual.

Do you want to be free? Then, believe in whatever you choose to believe in but do not believe that you are right and another person's belief is wrong. From this, conflict will end, wars will end, and devastation will end. And, we each will be allowed to experience mental freedom believing whatever it is we believe.

You Don't Have To Dig Too Deep

06/October/2014 07:22

I was cruisin' up Highway 101 a couple of weeks ago, flipping through the radio station, and I came upon this country station. The singer that was singing, sang a very profound lyric, *"You don't have to dig too deep to dig up dirt on me."*

Call it out. I love it!

I believe that most people in life are not about being holier than thou; on any level. They are simply about getting by and doing what they do. They are proud of their accomplishment and not ashamed of their improprieties.

Me too. Certainly, all of my deviations from the norm have been well documented in my literary writings.

Recently, I have been encountering a lot of people that are not of that mindset, however. Whether they be religious, academics, political, or simply attempting to project an image of all-knowing goodness, they attempt to hide, diminish, and cover-up all of their flaws and misdeeds. That is simply insincere.

Of course, there are some in this life who relish and relive all of their misdoings. They take pride in them. But, that is on the other end of the spectrum and not what I am discussing. I am talking about people trying to project an image of being more but not actually being more.

The fact is, attempting to be MORE is a very slippery slope. If you are <u>down</u>, then you have noting to prove. The moment you claim, *"More,"* then you can be toppled from your thrown.

Ultimately, what I am saying is be who you are. Own your actions. Choose to do what you choose to do, but then once it is done do not run from it. If you broken something, fix it. If you hurt someone, help him or her. If you just lived what you lived, out there in the allusive realms of suchness and reality, don't lie about it.

You are who you are. You are defined by what you did and what you do next. Own it.

Magical Thinking in the Modern Age

05/October/2014 17:26

I have been writing about the dangers of Magical Thinking for a lot of years now. How if you do this, if you believe that, all will be well with your life – you will achieve all of your desires.

This is just a salesman's ploy. A wandering salesman's snake oil, to get you to buy into their bullshit so they can make a dime.

How many Self-Help books have been written promising the same miraculous life changes if only you employee a recited, time-and-time-again, statement to, *"Be Positive," "Believe," I am this," I can control the mind of them," "I can focus and project my desired destiny,"* and the list goes on and on. Then, when it does not work out, there is always the catch phrase, written in small ink, *"It's because of you." "You didn't focus hard enough," You didn't try," "You are not pure enough,"* etc., etc., etc... Yet, the salesmen still get paid. Whether it be a book, a lecture, a whatever, you fork out your money and it is not their fault when you fail at what they promised. Stop the cycle!

If there is a fault, it is the fault with the soothsayers, promising you a reality that is out there... ...Out there... But, only if you do what they say. Out there... But, only if you concentrate hard enough and are pure enough.

But, the question must be asked, *"How pure are they?"* How pure and whole are they to be making money off of you? It sounds to me like you are already more than them because you have the money to fill their bank accounts. If they were all that; there would be no need for charging a fee.

It's like the psychic. Have you ever sat down with one? If you have an analytical mind, it is so easy to see through their game. The say, *"Some one in your family died and you were very upset..."* Okay, pretty much every one has had that experience. And, that is just one example of how they look at you, check out your clothing, your watch, your shoes, your style and quickly figure out what may be going on with you. What they are doing is, *"Fishing."* Fishing for your emotional center-point. If you say, *"No,"* to their question, they quickly fish a little further until they find something that you respond to. It is all psychological mind fuck and bullshit. Say, *"No,"* to them time and time again and see what they come up with.

As I have also stated forever... Look to the lives of these people – the people who propagate his style of deception. They are false. Have you actually met them? Have you actually spent time with them? Have you actually seen or heard how they behave in real life. If you had, I doubt that you would ever consider listening to what they have to say.

It is easy to believe in a person if you have not been allowed to see their idiosyncrasy. Stop believe in the liars who are only out there trying to make themselves seem to be more than you, while they ask you to pay them for their services. And, most of all, never forgive a person for their sins when they try to make up excuses about the flaws in their own personality, while still professing to be any sort of an anything.

If a person is telling you anything... Claiming to guide you... Professing to direct you... If they are not a proven and registered saint, they are a liar trying to make a living.

Life if a complex maze.

Truth is free.

The truth is based in simplicity and not desiring.

Here's some free advice (no charge) stop desiring what you desire and see how free your life will become.

People Quickly Forget

04/October/2014 23:10

Throughout the world there are tragedies that are taking place every moment. This has been the common course of history throughout time.

In, what has been deemed, *"The Civilized World,"* we forget this fact. We live in a fairly normal environment and are only confounded by the glitches in our day-to-day reality. Others across this planet are not so lucky, however. Whether it is the torture and devastation brought on by rulers like Pol Pot or Idi Amin or the devastation brought on by fanatical religious based groups like ISIS, pain, suffering, devastation, and hopelessness is prevalent at every moment in every time throughout history. Even, right now.

Do you ever think about this fact? Or, do you only think about whatever momentary reality you are engaged it?

If you have the time to focus on your moment reality, whatever your momentary reality may be, you are very blessed. Never forget this fact. Because there are more of the world's population focused on staying alive and survive through the devastation of torture than there are those who are allowed to feel okay and be upset when something is not going the way they believe that it should.

Stop being so selfish and so shortsighted. Stop thinking only about how you are feeling in any given moment. Care, and more importantly, do something positive. Never hurt anybody. Make this world a better place.

How Is Any Of That My Fault?

04/October/2014 20:51

Have you ever encountered a person who has wronged you – done something wrong that negatively affected you and then they got mad at you when you bring it to their attention?

Life is a selfish place. This is particularly the case when you encounter a selfish, self-absorbed person. They don't think about you or the effect they are having on you or on others. They simply do what they do, until they can do it no longer. Then, instead of offering an apology and trying to fix what they have broken they, quite often, try to turn it around on you. They try to blame you. They try to call attention to your concocted flaws – all in order to hide from their own culpability. You... The person who was injured by their actions in the first place.

Many people don't think unless they are forced to think. When they are forced to think they make excuses for their actions – they try to turn the blame in another direction away from themselves, so they can mentally try to hide from their karma. Many people do not even see the injury they are unleashing unless they are the one being injured. This is a very selfish mindset. But, it is the one employed by many people of this world. Don't be one of these people. Be more.

Publicity on the Sly

03/October/2014 13:41

The internet is a publicity seeker yellow brick road. Everything and everybody is on it. Some people go for the, *"Hey, look over here, it's me! Look at what I do!"* Others hide behind screen names and either try to praise or attack the thoughts and creations of others. Strange dichotomy... Strange condition...

What I forever find interesting are the people who go to the various sites that are in their field of work or in their field of interest and attempt to gain notoriety by making some statement about the something else of someone else. From this, I guess, they are trying to get their name out there as some sort of authority. Okay... But???

In life, it's all about the doing. Saying is not doing. Saying is just saying. I forever question what that equals. But, as has been proven in so many university based statistical studies, negativity spreads like wild fire across the internet; much more than positivity. Hating seems to be the common language. I guess that is because when you hate you get all fired-up with adrenalin, your blood pressure rises, and you feel like you have a cause. But, this junk is not a cause. It is not changing the world. It is just typing on some typing keys, trying to make yourself look like you know something. All this is very curious...

On the internet, I have noticed people that I have met, or even know, using their real name and photo; launching opinions, supporting stuff that is simply not founded in fact and in many cases, is just flat out ridiculous. ...Ridiculous, for anyone who actually checks the facts. Yet, they associate their name and face with it. They claim responsibility for their words.

Here's where the free publicity comes in. Your name... Your face... People have heard of you... But, at what cost?

For those of us who look to the bigger-picture in life, for those of us who try to understand psychological motivation and circumstance, I find all of this very interesting. For here is a person, I imagine they are not a bad person, yet they spread the virus of negativity as a means to get their name and face seen and known. Why? Why? Why?

If you base your reality upon attack, if you lend your name to criticism based in falsehoods and uninformed opinions, how does any of that leads to a better you? Let alone how does any of that lead to a better ALL? If your words are just words, attempting to lend a basis of fact to your personalized opinion – yes, it may lead to people knowing your name, (and maybe even your face), but shouldn't what you be known for and associated with be more than simply misguided rants based upon an unfounded personalization of reality? Shouldn't what you are known for be based on the good you have done, the good you have said, and the good you have personally created?

I believe in people. I think we should all be more than this. ...Be more than publicity seeking court jesters.

Karmic Intersections

03/October/2014 07:48

Out of the blue, we all bump into people we know from time to time. Sometimes it is people we are happy to see, sometimes it is not. But, unless there is some big unfolding event linked to this random human interaction, we pass these occurrences off to the chaos of life.

Sometimes, however, we may see a person more than once – see them in very difference circumstance. Then, it sets our mind to wondering, *"Why?"*

Here in a place like Los Angeles it is very common to see celebrities. You may drive past them in your car, walk past them on the street, you may find yourself sitting next to them in a restaurant, a bar, or a nightclub. It's not a big thing...

The only reason I mention celebrities is due to the fact that because they are celebrities you mentally take note of seeing them. The fact is, you may pass by the same person a million times and never even notice them. Unless they stand out from the crowd, you will not even make a mental note of seeing that person. And, here is where the mysticism is born. Some people you mentally take note of, most you do not. You may be next to the same person, in different environments, time-after-time, but neither of you will notice. Awh, the mysteries of life…

But, again, we come back to the question of, *"Why?"* *"Why do two people interact; intersect without the thought of ever doing so?"*

I think back to a time when my friend and I were leaving a nightclub and the director Robert Rodriguez was leaving at the same time. He bumped into me. No big thing... I just smiled and thought, *"Robert Rodriquez bumped into me."* A band called, *Tito and Tarantula* was playing. They are a band that Rodriquez has used to soundtrack several of his movies. They play good music. I originally used to see the lead singer of the band, Tito Larriva, (who is also commonly an actor in Rodriguez's films), back in the early days of punk when he was in a band called, *The Plugz*. Anyway, I went home and didn't think about the incident any more. The very next day, however, I was at, what was a GREAT music store in L.A., Virgin Records, on Sunset and Crescent Heights. I bought a couple CDs, got in the elevator to go to my car and in steps Robert Rodriguez. Did he notice me? I don't know. But, I did take note of him.

L.A. being what L.A. is, Psycho Stalker and Paparazzi Central, I did not speak with him. Didn't want to give him the wrong idea. But, it was a strange occurrence. And, it raises the question, *"Why?"*

I think back to a time several years before this occurrence. I had met this couple in Chengdu, in Central China. At the time, Chengdu was the only jumping off point to catch a flight into Lhasa; where we were both going. Once in Lhasa, as I was acclimatizing myself to the altitude so I could ride my bike off into the distance of Tibet, I hung out with the couple several times. He was a lawyer who had just graduated *Harvard Law School* and was on his way to a big New York firm after their vacation. Me, I had been living in Shanghai and was lamenting about a girl I had met that I had virtually no way of getting her free from the PRC.

In any case, a couple of months later, I was back in L.A. I had given up fighting the Dark Gods that rule China and had met another girl. We were walking hand-in-hand down a side street in Venice and I hear, *"Scott!"* It was that same couple on another vacation. They asked if this was the girl I had told them about, as she was also Chinese. It was not. This did piss her off a bit as she was a raging, jealous, very feisty woman. But, how could this happen – meeting on the other side of the world for no apparent reason in a totally random place in time? I don't know, but it did. I never saw them again… So what was the purpose of any of it?

In each of our lives, this type of thing goes on – as stated, maybe more often than we even realize. As I often refer to this fact, life is a strange puzzle. A puzzle we will never have the answer to. Though people will, no doubt, try to seek one out.

And, this is the thing… You can search. In fact, you can drive yourself mad searching for answers. But, at best, anything you come up with will only be a guess, as life was not ever meant to be understood.

For me, though I forever question occurrences, (that is simply my nature), I never let myself become lost in those questions. If I figure it out, great! But, most of the time, I do not.

Questing life can drive you insane.

Witnessing life, sets you free.

Your life. Your choice.

You Owe Me

02/October/2014 08:18

As we each live our way through life there are people who intersect with us that truly disrupt our flow. Some of these people we invite into our lives, most we do not. But, what comes from this intersection is a disruption of our evolution – our life happiness and our life contribution.

I believe, as we get older, most of us have encountered people that fall into this realm. People that are so involved with themselves that they do not even see the destruction that they are evoking to all of those around them.

The sad fact is, many of these people thrive on this destruction. They become empowered by it. They hear their name mentioned or they hear about the negative impact they are having and they feel the only sense of self and power that they have ever felt – as they are finally being acknowledged. Thus, they continue their negative actions.

I could provide a list of the negative actions that the people who inhabit this realm employee. But, we all know what they are. Simply look to a person who has hurt or disrupted your life and there is the definition.

A true person, a good person is never so self-involved that they damage the life or the lifetime of another. The mindless, however, go through life doing what they do, only thinking about self, and this is where all the problems begin.

In life, we will each encounter these types of people. Not good, but that is the way that it is. In some cases, they are right next to us, interactive with us, and their negativity, based in lies and deception, is so close that it haunts us. In other cases, they do their damage from afar. But, as is the case with all things – all beings in life, if they damage, if they destroy, if they do not think of others before they think of self, then any damage that they create will only come back to destroy them. This is why the truly conscious help rather that hurt, fix rather than break, repair rather than destroy.

Life is a complicate puzzle. But the fact is, those who hurt you, owe you. If they do not pay the price, don't worry; their own actions will seal their fate.

You Stole My Ideas

01/October/2014 08:47

In the modern world (particularly the world of the internet) there is a lot of thievery. Intellectual property theft, if you will... People read, watch, listen to the works created by others, take what they will from it, and then use it to their own ends.

Anyone who has created something – something unique and whole onto itself, understands how important that creation is. But... And, this is a big BUT, once the idea is out there, people (the uncreative) grab a-hold – they use the fundamentals and the foundations of and for that idea, put their own spin on it, and try to make it their own.

The fact of the matter is, most of the world is inhabited by the uncreative and the unmotivated. Though these people may have ideas, they never bring them to life. Then, there are those who do have the motivation. At least the motivation to piggy-back themselves onto the ideas and creations of others in order to get their name and their face out there and maybe even add a few digits to their bank account. These people use the words, the ideas, and the creations of others to make a name for themselves.

I always wondered how this type of person lives with themselves? But, that's just me. I guess they're getting their ego stroked and their bank accounts filled.

We are all shaped by our culture and the timeframe we live within. Though this is the obvious case, most of us, if we are truly creative, forge our own pathway to suchness. We don't steal the words, ideas, and creations of others in an attempt to add validity to our life.

I think if we look throughout history, we easily see that those who do the borrowing/the stealing do not ultimate emerge as the remembered. But, that history lesson does not take away the frustration for the truly creative living in a specific moment in time.

Say you own words. Create your own creations. And, stop stealing the ideas of others simply in an attempt to make yourself something more.

Wipe the slate clean. Begin anew. Form your own ideas. Use your own words. Create your own creations. The world will be a better place.

Removing the Layers

01/October/2014 08:01

I've been working on a new music collection. It's an abstract soundscape created entirely with vintage synthesizers.

I was taking some time to listen to one of the compositions yesterday and I was realizing how the essence of the piece was there but it had become very convoluted.

That's one of the things that has happened in this modern era of music. With the ability to lay track upon track, a lot of musical expressions can but put into one moment of music.

Certainly, it all began with Les Paul who was the first to record one piece of music and then simultaneously mix that piece onto tape with additional music he was playing live. From that sound-on-sound inception the ability to lay down multiple music tracks has continued to multiply: 4-track, 8-track, 16-track, 24-track, to now when you can lay down virtually unlimited tracks. There are some pieces of music that even I have created that have over a hundred tracks.

But, there I was, I knew I had something. I was not simply going to trash it. But, I had to find what was there – hidden among the many track. I began to mute the tracks, one by one. Finally, there it was, one tack, recorded in mono that was perfect. Whole and All onto itself.

This is a lot like life. So many things are going on in all of our lives that sometimes we get confused with what we really should be; need to be doing. At times, we really need to mute the chaos, become silent, and focus only on one track.

Say It In Your Autobiography

30/September/2014 09:03

You know, I always find it interesting when you pop around the internet and you read people's bio on their website and on other websites that talk about them. Ever since I wrote my first article and later a book, I found it very uncomfortable to read my bio. It felt like two things. One, it didn't really capture who I am. And two, it all sounded a little egotistical. This, even though someone else is writing it. I still feel that way.

Yes, yes, I know… There is the need to get the, *"Who you are out there,"* if you do anything for public consumption. …So people can get the gist of who and what you are. …What are your credentials to say or do anything. But, it is just weird.

Then, there are the haters. You pop around the various websites and you see all kinds of negativity about all kinds of people. Why? What does that prove?

Me, I always try to be very positive about a person. That is unless they have truly fucked with my life. Even then, I give them the benefit of the doubt as long as I can. But, hating on a person that you have not met or do not even know, that is simply foolish.

But, some people just hate. Some people are just negative. There may be a million reasons why. But, that is just not good.

I remember back when I was like in 7th grade, one of our assignments was to write a bio about our self – describing who and what we are. I remember many people didn't know. They talked about the color of their hair, what they liked to wear or do. Few discussed who they were and where they were going in life. That's natural, for sure… When you are so young the world is in front of you.

As you get older, you become defined. Defined by what you have done. Done… By hook or by crook. *"I am this,"* we exclaim. *"I am that." "I did this." "I did that."* But, so what…

The only reason to say we have done anything is so that we can do something more. And, the more we do one thing, the harder it is to do something else.

Just like the 7th grade assignment, you should write down what you are and how you view yourself and where you are going. See, how you see yourself. It may be very revealing.

No Truth

30/September/2014 08:13

I was kicking around one of my favorite bookshops yesterday. There was an elderly lady stocking the shelves while speaking to another customer. She said, *"I don't think that there's much truth in these books or there wouldn't be so many of them being written."* This made me smile.

I'll just leave it at that. Perfect truth in perfect words.

Other People's Words and the Path of Focused Anger
29/September/2014 13:33

Recently, I was asked to preform a role in an upcoming film. As you may imagine, I get asked to be in a lot of movies. Most of the rolls I turn down; jokingly stating, *"The only bad movies I'm in are my own."* But, every now and then I get offered something that really sparks my interest; like this one.

This film is a dialogue-driven drama. My character in the film is a very angry guy. Angry... That is what caught my interest.

As I have been running my lines, preparing for the film, it has been very interesting to see how memorizing the anger-based words, written by another person, and then voicing them – bringing them into my own psyche, can really effect the mood and energy of all things around me.

Anger is a strange emotion... We all feel it, (from time to time). But, it is what we do with it that defines our life.

Certainly, in times gone past, it was easiest to just go up and knock somebody out when you were pissed off at them. But, times have changed. The world has gotten so litigious. You just can't do that kind of stuff anymore.

As someone who works out and teaches the fighting arts, in one way or another, virtually every day of my life, I have long studied and charted the roots of anger and how it effects physical interactions. That being stated, it is really interesting to see how being angry as a character, even when I am practicing for the role, can really affect my inner being.

As a filmmaker and an actor, I have long witness how some people really get into their roles when they are supposed to be angry. I have seen actors break things, shove people down, or even hit them. I guess, *"The Method,"* people would claim that person was totally in their moment. But... It's just a job. It's not real life... Control yourself!

I was watching this season's finale of the *Showtime* series, *Ray Donovan*, last night. Though I have not personally met him, the star of the show, Liev Schreiber, and I have a close connection in that he spent some time growing up at the ashram of my guru, Swami Satchidananda. Anyway...

During this season, one of the sub-characters was this Self-Help, New Age Guru guy. Now, we all know what I think about that kind of a person, so I won't go into it here. His character did what they all do, spitting out all of the regurgitated words that have been spoken over-and-over again. The character was very successful at it, however, equally millions and millions of dollars. I believe if there is a judgment of excellence in that field, that is it; financial success; i.e.: Tony Robbins and Deepak Chopra. Everyone else is just a wantabe. Anyway… Full of himself, his character had no limits, felt universally empowered to do whatever he felt like doing, and ended up killing another character. Here lies the point: empowerment, power, unbridled success, and generated anger can equal just that, the hurting and/or killing of another person.

For what does unleashed anger equal? Destruction, injury, murder, death.

So, though it is fun for me to play this character and spit out some negative, angry words, I never let it overpower me. In fact, it is especially nice for me as it is someone else's production, so I don't have to do everything on the set, like I do in my *Zen Films…* I just get to show up and talk.

It is kind of like the best known Tibetan Buddhist actor, Richard Gere, once said when asked about some of the off beat characters he has played, *"It's fun…"* And, that's just it. It's not fun to be angry. But, it's fun to play angry.

Only get angry in the realms of pretend.

Stirring the Pot

29/September/2014 08:06

There are some people who like to create controversy and disharmony. I believe that we have all met people like this. The say things and do things that are either distorted or not true simply to get people to believe things about life-situations or other people in order to cause them to become angry at that situation or that person. Some call this practice backstabbing but it is actually much deeper than this.

The reason that people commonly behave in this matter is that they hold a low sense of self-worth. Where this comes from can be anybody's guess. But, early in life they have discovered that they can gain a false sense of control over others by guiding them with misinformation and/or lies. The result of this type of behavior causes all kinds of interpersonal disharmonies that can lead to confrontations, arguments, fights, and on a larger scale, wars.

The problem with people who behave in this manner is that the people they are telling their stories to commonly are not aware that they are being lied to and strung along in order for the person to gain a sense of control and self-worth. In other words, people believe the lies.

I believe that most of us want to trust people and believe the things that we are told are true and valid. It is human nature to believe that others are the same as us – speaking the facts, as we know them. It is only after encountering people of the aforementioned type that we then begin to become less trusting and are forced to begin to critically analyze the words of others before we move forward with what we have heard.

From a person perspective, my friend and *Zen Filmmaking* associate, Donald G. Jackson, was notorious for this type of behavior. He would tell people all kinds of things about other people, simply to get a rise out of them. He would, in fact, totally break apart film production teams simply to satisfy his need to gain misguided control. There was several times when I was associated with him that people I considered friends would either shun me or accost me due to false words that Jackson had spoken. It was very strange.

For me, I saw through this character flaw early on and, as such, took his words with a grain of salt. I heard them but I did not allow them to influence me as to my judgment of a person's actual personality. Sadly, other people were not so astute and, as such, he caused our relationships to fall apart.

He was the only person I ever knowingly hung out with who behaved in this manner. Though many times it did cause friction in our friendship.

The causation factor for this type of behavior is rooted in a person's desire for power, dominance, and control. You can commonly see this type of behavior in the workplace when something has gone awry and higher management challenges middle management as to their actual management skills. From this challenge, the person in middle management begins to take out their lack of control on their underlings. They shift the blame, they blame others, they may even make up lies about their coworkers in order to shift responsibility, but the outcome of this style of human interaction is all the same – they have created disharmony due to the fact that they are not whole, confident, responsible for their actions, and complete onto themselves. Thus, they create havoc in order to shift the focus from their own inabilities to manage towards someone else. This type of behavior is commonly titled, *"Saving their own ass."*

Ultimately, (and perhaps sadly), we are all going to be forced to interact with this type of person as we pass through life. There is no way around it. In fact, in the workplace environment, this type of person may actually have a certain amount of control over us. But... We do not have to let this type of person control who we are, how we feel about ourselves, and how we make our life decisions about others.

We must each listen to all that we hear and then make our own choices about the truth and/or validity about what is spoken to us. Then, we must move forward, without judging, and make our own decision about people and this life-place free from the domination and control imparted by the words spoken by others.

Life is full of many people who embrace low human consciousness. In fact, we are more likely to encounter that type of person than one who actually embraces refined higher consciousness. This is life and that's the dilemma. But, by being whole and true onto ourselves, we can exist in a space of peace, knowing that we embrace the truth and are not dominated by the psychological inadequacies of others.

Be silent. Don't try to control or alter the consciousness and understandings of others. Don't desire control or admiration. And, this world becomes such a better place.

Finding the Opening

19/September/2014 13:29

When it comes to physical combat most people go at it with uncontrolled swinging fists and kicking legs. Even people who have rudimentarily trained in the fighting arts, many times, will quickly forget all that they have learned and simply try to survive the fight.

There is a small breed of people who actually like to fight. They enjoy the intended dominance over others and they may even like the pain of receiving the punch. This is a very small breed, however. These are people who live their life at a very animalistic level.

The fact of the matter is, mankind has not progressed very far in term of raising human consciousness over the past several millenniums. This, even though there are a fairly large number of people who focus their lives upon the spiritual aspects of existence. But, this has been the case forever. There have always been those whose minds veer towards the cosmic. The problem is, there are far more who focus upon conquest and dominance.

Though the spiritually inclined will deny this fact, at the root of mankind is violence – the overpowering of others to obtain what one wants. This is not right, nor is it the way it should be, but it is the way it is.

With this as a basis of understanding, we as martial artists must look to the refined realms of self-defense if we are ever drawn into a physical confrontation. Certainly there is the, *"First-Strike, Best-Strike Philosophy."* But, more than simply hitting him before he hits you, you must refine your understanding of physical combat, as the First Strike Philosophy may not always be applicable. Therefore, you must refine your mental understandings if you hope to remain unscathed in a physical confrontation.

It is important to note, even if you are a highly trainer fighter, you can be defeated – as has been proven time and time again. For this reason, you must never simply assume you will emerge victorious in a fight simply because you are bigger than your opponent or more highly trained. Additionally, in a competition setting you may find yourself tantalizing the audience by going round-for-round and elongating the time in the ring. But, on the streets it should never be like that. A street fight is won or lost very quickly and if you toy with or underestimate your opponent you will sooner or later get hit and that hit may debilitate you. To this end, and to elevate all of the unnecessary punch-for-punch mentality of a street fight, a true martial artist seeks the best and most rapid way to penetrate their opponent's defenses and defeat them.

One of the best ways to achieve this is to find an opening in your opponent's defenses. Highly trained boxers are very good at this, they look for an opening and then BAM, they punch through that hole. In many traditional martial art systems the student is not trained to be aware of these openings in their opponent's stances, however. They are simply taught to punch, kick, throw, and if they find themselves being punched or kicked at, to forcefully block that attack. Though this style of self-defense may work in certain circumstances, it may also prove to be a person's demise. Thus, a true martial artist must always study their opponent and then strikeout in the most rapid and effective manner possible.

The fact is, a street fight takes place in a few moments. Therefore, a long process of studying your opponent is generally not possible as is the case in the ring. To this end, you need to develop your ability to rapidly access your attacker and then deliver the most appropriate and devastating offense possible through the hole in their defenses. This is where opponent training and sparring in your school becomes essential. For in these controlled environments, once you have focused your understanding and know what you should be looking for, you can then develop the ability to see the opening and to rapidly penetrate your opponent's defenses, delivering a powerful attack.

For each system of the fighting arts the students are trained in a specific format of techniques. Though in school practice some of them look very pretty, i.e., the throws of Hapkido and Aikido. In actual combat, however, these types of techniques virtually never work, as they are far too elaborate. To this end, it is very important that you do not fool yourself into believe that simply because your training partner allows you to throw him in the gym that on the street this same type of technique will be a viable method of self-defense.

It is a simply fact of combat, the fighting techniques that work best on the street are those that are very direct, very powerful, and very simple to unleash. Whether this is a straight punch, front kick, or joint lock, the main thing to remember is that you want to see the opening and immediately strike through that opening. Don't wait because in street combat those opening are only there for a moment and that chance may not present itself again.

When you find that opening on your opponent and strike one of the main things that you must keep in mind is that it may not be effective. Never believe that one technique will be enough. Perhaps you did not strike hard enough, perhaps you opponent shifted his positing or moved, or perhaps your attack was blocked. The moment you realize that your attack was unsuccessful, you must immediately move and continue forward with additional defense, followed by offense. Never wait or you may not have the chance to relaunch your attack.

In the martial arts and, in fact, all fighting arts, the first thing the student must do is to master the techniques of the style they are studying. Once this has been accomplished you must then begin to study, understand, and anticipate the movements of your opponent. For what is martial art training if it is not gaining the developed knowledge to emerge successful from physical combat? To this end, never see your techniques as the sole end in physical combat. Instead, see them as a means to strikeout if you are attacked – using them to penetrating the defenses of your opponent and emerge victorious from any confrontation.

Study the subtleties of combat.

Child Punishment or Child Abuse

18/September/2014 08:20

I believe that we live in a very interesting time. Like the ancient Chinese curse states, *"May you live in interesting times."*

If you have been watching the news one of the big things going on right now is about this one NFL player who disciplined his kid with a small tree branch – know colloquially as a switch and left a few small open wounds on his legs. He has been suspended from his team and may face criminal charges. Discussions about this have been all over the news and talked about by the talking heads on CNN and all the other stations. I believe the one former sports star turned commentator said it best, when he stated in essence, *"If you make that a crime every African-American in the South will be going to jail."* And, when players from the man's team were interviewed they all stated that they had gotten worse than that. Me too.

On Anderson Cooper's show last night a woman was interviewed and she discussed how she would take her kids into the closet and hit them with a belt when they were bad. Her mother stated she would, *"Tear up the legs,"* (with a switch) when her daughter was bad.

When I was growing up, I was never hit with a switch. A belt, coat hanger, brush, or a good smack in the mouth was the weapon of choice employed by my parents. The African-American kids I went to school with would, however, show up with similar switch injures as the one currently being displayed on TV.

As time has gone on, most parents I know don't use weapons for discipline anymore. Say, twenty or twenty-five years ago, I watched as my friends who had kids would just spank them. Now, the parents of young children I know are all about the no physical discipline at all. ...Make the kids understand that they are doing something wrong by words but nothing physical.

From a psychological standpoint it has been studied that children who were physically discipline are more prone to being abusive to others, depressed, and hold onto a mindset of violence. Yeah... Maybe... But, for the generation upon generation of children who were physically disciplined, they too lived through their life.

Human consciousness always evolves. We, as human beings, do what we do, guided by what we have learned from our parents and our culture. But, at the end of the day, it is easy to judge but hard to change the world. And who among us possessed the ultimate knowledge to know what is absolutely right or absolutely wrong? It is all a point of view and a choice...

Michael Moore and the Cult of Negativity
17/September/2014 13:49

First of all, I must state, ever since Michael Moore began his career with *Roger and Me* and projects like his TV series, *TV Nation,* I have liked what he has done. It is no secret that I am a bleeding heart liberal and the swipes he has taken at Corporate American and the Republican Right have been appreciate – at least by me. Recently, however, he has been making a number of very negative comments about Obama. I'm not going to list them here as they are easily found on the internet. But, I believe this is just wrong.

Has Obama been the president of *Hope* and *Change* that I hoped he would be? No, no yet, anyway.... But, we must understand that the U.S. President is not an entity whole and complete onto himself. There are checks and balances that the President must go through. And, he has been held back by the Republican masses in the government.

Is this based, at least in part, on race? Yes, I believe that it is. No matter how much people claim that they are not/no-longer racist, this is just not the truth. Race runs through everything in America. Not just from the Caucasian perspective, but from the African-American, Latino, and Asian perspective, as well.

We must remember that Obama is half white. But, as one of my Black friends told me, *"If any color is running through your veins, that is how you will be seen."*

Anyway... To Michael Moore. Though I have liked the work Moore has done, there is one common theme that runs through everything he creates; namely his works attack a specific person or element of the life that we live.

It must be understood that attack is always based upon negativity. And, negativity never leads to positivity. It may lead to change, but it never leads to positivity. And positivity is never born from negativity. So, no matter how much I (and other people) like Moore's work, the source for his creation is focusing on a negative element of a person or of life and then going after it and exposing it.

As Michael Moore is obvious an intelligent, thought-full person, I have been very surprised that he is going after

Obama. Knowing the chaos Obama was handed when he became President and the hoops he has had to jump through to get anything done, I am very surprised that Moore would be focusing his negativity upon a man that has tried to make things better. And, maybe, in some small way, he has.

If we want All-Things to get better we must let go of negativity on all levels and focus only on the positive.

Enter the Dragon

16/September/2014 17:13

I was just reading a posting that Spike Lee is going to direct a new version of, *Enter the Dragon.* It will star Ken Yeong in the Bruce Lee role and Billy Bob Thornton will play, Ropper, the John Saxon role.

I think we all can agree that *Enter the Dragon* was and is the best English language martial arts film ever made. There have been a few good ones that followed like, *The Last Dragon* and *Big Trouble in Little China.* Even the comedies *Kentucky Fried Movie* and *They Call Me Bruce,* (for the few of us who know about those films), were pretty good. But, none have ever been as great as *Enter the Dragon.*

I'm a fan of Spike Lee and I like the work of Ken Yeong. Billy Bob Thornton... Well, he does what he does. In fact, way back, in the way back when, my bud Saturday Jim and I used to get pizzas from him at the pizza parlor he worked at in Hollywood. We would go in and order a large pizza each, a pitcher of beer each, and then we would go ride our motorcycles. But, that was a long-long-long time ago.

Now, I have a certain distant connection to *Enter the Dragon.* Thanks to my Co-Producer Kenneth H. Kim, who worked with the man, we cast my *Zen Film, Atomic Samurai* AKA *Samurai Johnny Frankenstein* in the offices of the producer of *Enter the Dragon,* Fred Weintraub.

All this being said, and let me get to the point... Though it is obviously intended to be a satire... Spike, don't do it! Don't kill the vision and/or the memory of the best martial art film ever made.

An Over Exaggerated Since of Self-Worth
16/September/2014 16:03

There is this library close to where I live. I go there all the time. I don't go there to check out books but because they have this GREAT used book section down in the garage. People donate books and they sell 'em. I continue to find great works of awesome reading.

Today, I go in to check out the books. Overpowering the entire environment is this guy (loudly) talking on his cell phone. He is telling someone on the other end of the line about this and about that – how he should be treating a family-member and how he should be sending him to therapy.

Now, I don't know if this guy is some sort of medical professional, shrink, or just a fucking loud mouth full of an over exaggerated sense of self-worth. But, this is a library okay. And, aren't you supposed to be quiet in a library?

I don't know... In place like (here) L.A. you get a loud of these loud mouth assholes who think they have something to tell the world. And, you even have a certain amount of foolish people who listen to them. I guess the listeners believe because the person is talking so loud and telling them what to do, that they must have something worth listening to.

But, it is just like the fact that the same self-help book has been written over and over and over again – saying the same thing. ...Just like the people who steal those stolen words and say them over and over and over again. Is any of this helping anyone? No. People still suffer from the same symptoms. At best, the words only stroking the ego of those who write them and those who speak them.

Be whole onto yourself and you are free. And, never overpower anyone else's space by being a loud-mouthed asshole full of an exaggerated sense of self-worth because then you just show that you are not even aware enough about the space of others to be worthy of saying anything.

The Pinocchio Syndrome

16/September/2014 16:03

There is this commercial running on television now where the basic joking statement of it is, *"Did you know that Pinocchio was a bad motivational speaker?"* The commercial then shift to the wooden figure of Pinocchio in front of a crowd, telling those in attendance that they can be winners. The camera then goes to this guy who is sitting in the audience and is obviously a loser. The more Pinocchio tells him (and them) that they can be winners, the longer his nose grows. This is an ideal depiction of so many of the self-help gurus out there who are simply lying to their audience.

First of all, the self-help guru himself or herself is lying in the fact that they are telling anyone how they can or should be. Who are they to tell anyone anything? For the most part, these self-help teachers are some of the lowest level people inhabiting this earth. For if they were true in their message they would be speaking for free, not charging their audience, and they would not be stealing the words of those who have actually achieved something with their life. They would be saying something organic and self-realized. Instead, they heard something somewhere from someone and they are repeating it and claiming it as their own.

Furthermore, people who are seekers lock themselves into the mindset of seeking. They have already decided that they are not enough – that they are not whole onto themselves. From this mindset they feed the ego driven mind, based upon a framework of insecurity, that these motivational speakers dwell within. How can you learn from a person who has no personal realization of their own? With no person realization all they speak is lies.

Think for yourself. Make yourself something MORE.

The Scott Shaw Zen Blog 4.0

16/September/2014 15:47

Hey Everyone,

Okay, I'm back. Thanks for all of the requests for me to get the blog back up and running.

A funny story… Today, just as I was sitting back to an afternoon latte' at *Starbucks,* eating some of their very good popcorn, the thought of re-starting the blog came to mind. Just then, a girl walks by with the word, *"Blog,"* across the back of her tee shirt. It made me smile.

Can't fight the signs, I guess… :-)

I'm still pretty busy on a few projects, so this version of the blog will probably not be as dense as the previous blog(s) – at least not for right now. And, I am going to change things up a bit.

Previously, the *Scott Shaw Zen Blogs* were made up of (solely) essays. I'm going to do things a little different this time. The *Scott Shaw Zen Blog 4.0* will be a combination of essays, brief thoughts, and some photos.

Note: You can find the thoughts and aphorisms that were presented in the Scott Shaw Zen Blog 4.0 in the book, Zen Mind Life Thoughts.

Now, I am not so vain as to be one of those people into taking selfies. Nor, do I like to look at myself that much. :-) But, sometimes a photo can equal a thousand words. So, in this version of the blog I'll let you see a bit of what I'm seeing and what I doing.

So, I'll start this blog off with a few photos taken over the past couple of months, (when the blog was down), and a couple of writing(s).

Scott Shaw Books-in-Print

*About Peace: A 108 Ways to Be At Peace
   When Things Are Out of Control*
Advanced Taekwondo
Arc Left from Istanbul
Ballet for a Funeral
Bangkok and the Nights of Drunken Stupor
Bangkok: Beyond the Buddha
Bus Ride(s)
Cairo: Before the Aftermath
*Cambodian Refugees in Long Beach, California:
   The Definitive Study*
Chi Kung For Beginners
China Deep
Echoes from Hell
Essence: The Zen of Everything
e.q.
Guangzhou: A Photographic Exploration
Hapkido: Articles on Self-Defense: Volume 1
Hapkido: Articles on Self-Defense: Volume 2
Hapkido: Essays on Self-Defense
Hapkido: The Korean Art of Self-Defense
Hong Kong: Out of Focus
Independent Filmmaking: Secrets of the Craft
In the Foreboding Shadows of Holiness
Israel in the Oblique
Junk: The Backstreets of Bangkok
*Last Will and Testament According to the
   Divine Rites of the Drug Cocaine*
L.A.: Tales from the Suburban Side of Hell
Los Angeles Skidrow: 1983
*Marguerite Duras and Charles Bukowski:
   The Yin and Yang of Modern Erotic Literature*
Mastering Health: The A to Z of Chi Kung
Nirvana in a Nutshell
On the Hard Edge of Hollywood
Pagan, Burma: Shadows of the Stupa
*Sake' in a Glass, Sushi with Your Fingers:
   Fifteen Minutes in Tokyo*

Scream of the Buddha
Scream: Southeast Asia and the Dream
Scribbles on the Restroom Wall
Samurai Zen
Sedona: Realm of the Vortex
Shama Baba
Shanghai Whispers Shanghai Screams
Shattered Thoughts
Singaore: Off Center
South Korea in a Blur
Suicide Slowly
Taekwondo Basics
Ten to Thirty
The Chronicles: Zen Ramblings from the Internet
The Ki Process: Korean Secrets for Cultivating Dynamic Energy
The Little Book of Yoga Breathing
The Little Book of Zen Mediation
The Lyrics
The Most Beautiful Woman in Shanghai
The Passionate Kiss of Illusion
The Screenplays
The Tao of Chi
The Tao of Self Defense
The Voodoo Buddha
The Warrior is Silent: Martial Arts and the Spiritual Path
The Zen of Modern Life and the Reality of Reality
TKO: Lost Nights in Tokyo
Urban India: Bombay, Delhi, Lucknow
Varanasi and Bodhi Gaya: Shade of the Bodhi Tree
Wet Dreams and Placid Silence
Woods in the Wind
Yoga: A Spiritual Guidebook
Yosemite: End of the Winter
Zen and Modern Consciousness
Zen Buddhism: The Pathway to Nirvana
Zen Filmmaking
Zen in the Blink of an Eye
Zen O'clock: Time to Be
Zen: Tales from the Journey
Zero One